G000245436

Macc and the Art of Long Distance Walking

Graham Wilson

Macc and the Art of Long Distance Walking

with illustrations by Gerry Dale

Millrace

Published in Great Britain in May 1998 by
Millrace
2a Leafield Road, Disley
Cheshire SK12 2JF

Reprinted October 1998

ISBN: 1 902173 01 5

Printed and bound in Great Britain by
Bookcraft (Bath) Ltd, Midsomer Norton, Avon

Acknowledgements

The author would like to thank the following for permission to use extracts reproduced in this book: The Climbers' Club (articles by Menlove Edwards in CC Journals), The Fell & Rock Climbing Club of the English Lake District (articles by Katherine Hopkinson and Bentley Beetham in F&RCC Journals), Victor Gollancz (*One Man's Mountains,* Tom Patey), Anne Murray (*Mountaineering in Scotland,* W H Murray), The Rucksack Club (articles by Eustace Thomas and S Forrester in RC Journals) and The Scottish Mountaineering Club (extract from the SMC Glencoe and Ardgour Climbers' Guide).

Contents

Preface

'You look a little shy; let me introduce you
to that leg of mutton,' said the Red Queen.
'Alice - Mutton; Mutton - Alice.'
(Through the Looking Glass)

As we are into introductions, let us introduce you to three pertinent questions:

Macc? What Art? Where are the Maps?

Macc?

Macc is also a curious place. Its Sunday name is Macclesfield but it is known, at least to those who who live there, as Macc. The football team is Macc Town, the local paper is *The Macc Times* and the members of the somewhat scurrilous pop group are the Macc Lads. Such is the extent of this abbreviated use that the most prestigious hotel with its revolving door, art deco bar and 'Can I take your coat, Sir?' could not sustain the indignity of being called The Macc Arms and went into terminal decline. The authentic pronunciation is a slight glottal stop between Macc and the noun that follows. This is not the case if Macc follows the noun. Here the speaker should effect an elision between the two parts. A good example is the local school which, to distinguish it from those of Canterbury, Worcester and other educational experiments perpetrated by Edward VI, may be known, on headed notepaper, as The King's School in Macclesfield but, universally, to the real world as Kings*m*acc.

Another curious fact is that it does not conform to that relatively exact science known as Market Demography. According to the figures, the town should be an ideal location for fast developing entrepreneurs. The Captains of Private Enterprise set up their stalls, wait for the windfall and then some little while later fold their tents and steal sheepishly away. Macclesfield is conservative with a small 'c'. Although it is not curious that Macclesfield, given its constituency, is Conservative in the present day, it is odd that a mill town with a substantial working class also voted Tory before the arrival of Middle England. The explanation is that the area was a traditional Liberal stronghold. The masters voted Liberal so the anti-vote was Tory. The demise of Asquith and Lloyd George and the rise of Socialism seem to have passed the place and people by and in consequence no one bothered to change the voting habits of several generations.

And there are advantages in the fact that the town would not know a bandwagon if it saw one. Whereas most places in the Sixties decided to finish the job for the Luftwaffe and demolish their centres to install the obligatory malls and walkways, Macclesfield for the most part left well alone. Whether the action or otherwise of the Town Elders was prescient or dilatory is hard to say, but the outcome is that many interesting buildings, ranging from weavers' cottages to the silk masters' town houses, were spared the chain and ball of demolition and much of the town has been carefully restored. Of course, Planning by Procrastination has its down-side. The inner relief road spent the early part of its life as a cul-de-sac and the new bypass leaps and bounds towards the town with all the confidence of an Olympic Triple Jumper, only to stumble on the take-off board and collapse in a heap on one of the more congested streets in the borough.

But that's Macclesfield. Flat Macc - take it or leave it. Not that it is short of its quota of bumps and hollows but it was flat enough to act as the fulcrum for the canal and rail systems that stretch from Manchester to the Potteries and this plays an important part in the following narrative. But it is really a step. A step up from the Cheshire Plain. This leads to a final curious thing. When many people come to Macclesfield, they initially see it as a step, a stepping-stone in their march through life. Thirty years later, they are somewhat surprised to find that they have set up camp in the middle of the river. There are probably many reasons for this: the proximity of Manchester and its airport; the accessibility of the motorway system; the quick train to London. But for me and, I suspect, a good few others, the fact that there are hills beyond the door of this particular step may not be irrelevant.

This brings us to the current link that Macclesfield has with the historical growth of walking in the Peak District, a growth that stemmed from the proximity of industrial cities and towns both to east and west. What had been a steady trickle of enthusiasts up to the First World War turned into the torrent unleashed by the mass unemployment of the Depression. Men and women travelled by bus, tram and train, or often by foot, out of Sheffield and Manchester into what must have been the therapeutic atmosphere of Derbyshire's Crag and Moorland. The tradition was to walk from the outside in, explore and then walk out, rather than, as is the custom today, drive into the middle, park by a picnic table and follow some Nature Trail laid out by a friendly Park Ranger. So, as it seems odd that the town-dweller who claims the countryside as the lung of his existence should spend a significant part of his recreational activity polluting the dales with carbon emissions, there is something to be said for a return to past practice. Macclesfield has a train station; travel by rail and enter the Peak from there. In addition, the old rail and water routes are now given over to leisure, and the former Macclesfield, Bollington & Marple railway line and the adjacent section of the Cheshire Ring offer convenient entries and exits to and from the foothills.

If, then, you look carefully at the map, you will see the hills overlooking Macclesfield fold back in waves of ever increasing height and complexity. First, the immediate skyline ridge stretching from White Nancy to Croker Hill; second, a round that sweeps from Lyme Park across to The Cat and Fiddle and down the land above Dane Bower from which flow the waters that will eventually empty into the Trent; and third, the Edges of Burbage, Axe and Wolf which bound the gritstone world of the Dark Peak from the limestone of the White. This configuration allows walks of increasing distance and seriousness to be planned and undertaken and Part One of the book suggests five such possibilities.

Finally, Macclesfield has a lot of pubs. From the station alone, five are immediately visible, each selling a different variety of real bitter ale. Indeed, it has to be confessed that the number exceeds any reasonable need, in that there is more than one occasion where the proximity of the establishments is such that you have scarcely to leave go of the apron strings of one before you can clutch the skirts of another.

What Art?

A dictionary definition of the term seems to divide it into two distinct categories: Art in the sense of a skill and Art in the sense of a concept or idea. As the acquisition of the skill of walking is beyond memory and it can only be improved through practice on rough or steep ground, there seems little point in pursuing this line of defence to justify the use of the term in the title.

It is rather the concept of long distance walking which is worth examining and the idea of the following pages is to see what you can get out of walking in addition to blisters and a good appetite. There appear to be two main types: through-routes that get from A to B in an efficient manner and walks that aim to cover a considerable amount of ground by following some natural or logical course.

A good example of the former is to look at Sheet 33 of the OS Landranger Series of Great Britain and imagine that you want to travel from Kinloch Hourn to Arnisdale. By foot you would set off in the logical north-westerly direction and arrive after walking for eight miles by track and path through Glen Dubh Lochain; by car you motor east along a single-track road, off the edge of the map, on to Sheet 34 until you reach the A87 just short of Invergarry; you then double back on yourself past Clunie (back on to Sheet 33), through Glen Shiel behind that Skyebound scourge of Scotland, the touring caravan, up and over the tortuous single-track road from Ratagan and along the coastlines of the Sound of Sleat and Loch Hourn to your desired destination, a distance of some seventy miles. With luck, a car might arrive before the leisurely walker. It would be more interesting as a race between the pedestrian tortoise and the motorised hare if two separate parties were to start at Inverie, one boarding the ferry to collect their car at Mallaig, the other setting off over Mam Barrasdale, both with the same destination of Arnisdale in mind.

I chose this example to tempt you to look at the relevant map that covers the finest area of Britain. At one time, the whole of the country must have been covered by such through-routes. The internet of drove roads, coffin tracks and sunken lanes has undoubtedly shrunk but some remain and there is a sentimental pleasure in hearing in the sound of your footfall the echo of those that have passed before.

The second type is the constructed challenge. At times this might follow an obvious feature or series of features; at others it might be connected by a series of coincidental points on the ground, eg all hills over *x* feet in the county of Peakshire. In particular, the round where you can see where you are going and where you have been is pleasing and to complete the walk in the terms you set yourself is a great source of satisfaction. The scale of the British countryside is conducive to this type of activity; it is not especially difficult to walk in a day from one end of the Lake District to the other or, if you choose the right point, to traverse the mainland of Scotland, and a long distance walk enables you to hold that part of the country in the hollow of the mind's eye and allows you to feel that you have really got to know at least one portion of the land you live in.

To score a debating point, it is tempting to dress up this concept in metaphysical clothing. Climbing literature has its fair share of mystic happening and quasi-religious explanation of the mountain experience. However the reality is often less uplifting. When struggling over the peat groughs of Bleaklow in mist and rain one tends to think less of Ruskin's dictum that 'Mountains are the beginning and the end of all natural scenery' but rather more an old countryman's dismissive remark when asked his views after being taken on a tour of the scenic Lake District:

'Why, it's nobbut stanes and watter.'

Where are the Maps?

As has been suggested, one point of long distance walking is the particular relationship developed between the individual and the ground that he covers. For this reason, I never intended to produce a guide of the 'turn left at the third sheep on the right' variety. Instead, I am confident that Gerry Dale's eye-relief illustrations give a sense of what is involved. The guide assumes a competence and interest in map-reading and has no wish to drive the reader along ever deepening ways and trails. (Rumour has it that the Countryside Commission are considering erecting elevated look-out platforms at certain strategic points on the Pennine Way.) The idea is that, as the walks that follow in Part One touch and cross each other, you can, if you wish, shake the kaleidoscope and follow any pattern that might emerge. Those that appear in Part Two are more serious and probably require a less cavalier attitude.

One

The Midgrit Trail

The start of this route is the Middlewood Way and the Middlewood Way starts in Macclesfield. True to form, the town does not let itself down. It is no leafy lane that sets the traveller on his path but a sign outside the railway station that in no uncertain manner points the way towards what appears to be a dingy dead-end of rail and road arches. You stiffen the sinews, pass through this complex, skirt the River Bollin (not yet the riparian idyll promised in the leaflets of the Countryside Management Service) and after negotiating a couple of zebra crossings, nip round the back of Tesco's. Before you know it, you have passed back under the Silk Road via the local, but as yet uncommissioned, Art Gallery and on to a connecting series of cycle tracks and dog- (and, for all I know, cat-) walks that bound the Tytherington Estate. The green stuff on either side is grass. Continue, keeping an eye out for pandas, until you arrive at a fine wooden bridge (OS SJ 925759), the alpha and omega of this and other expeditions. It is a sad reflection on a nation that had the engineers and craftsmen to span Sydney Harbour and construct countless wooden artefacts of every shape and size, that it has so degenerated into a farrago of land speculators and burger franchisees that the bridge had to be built in Holland.

If this is not to your taste, you can avoid it completely by parking as near to the Dutch Bridge as is convenient (the former Rugby Club will do) or walking up the Buxton Road and joining the canal at (or after) The Puss in Boots, from where a short stroll will join the same starting point. But there is no light without shade and if you do start at the official beginning, you will have a reminder, albeit fleeting, of the industrial wasteland that choked the life out of previous generations and drove them to demand the freedom to roam that you nowadays take for granted.

Either way, on the next leg to the former station at Higher Poynton a choice is available. You can cross the bridge, turn left and stride manfully up the slight gradient of the Middlewood Way or continue on the canal, flat and meandering. The best choice is to combine the two, as they often converge. If you choose to continue up the disused railway track, you will be following the line of the former Macclesfield, Bollington & Marple Railway, opened in 1869 after the usual scuffle and squabbling that seemed to be an essential ingredient when a town was in the grip of 'rail fever'. Local worthies, Vernon of Poynton and Arighi of Macclesfield, seemed to be among the principal objectors but the promise to the former of the construction of a siding (with suitable compensation) towards Park Pit and the settlement of £1,650 to the latter seem to have reduced the insuperable difficulties to manageable proportions. You will, moreover, be following the trail of what was known affectionately, or otherwise, as the 'Bollington Bug'. This, a petrol electric railcar, was commissioned to carry mill workers between Macclesfield and Bollington, leaving Bollington at 7.23 am and, after thirteen shuttles, finally returning at 10.45 pm. The only exception to this was a late service on Saturday night that was extended to Poynton, enabling the Poyntonians to enjoy the excitement of a night out in Macclesfield.

There are, no doubt, those who feel that walking up a cutting offers little in the way of challenge or scenery and they would be right. However, if deserted, as this section often is, it has an Other World feel to it that is a little reminiscent of George Orwell's description in *The Road to Wigan Pier* of the juxtaposition of the miners underground and those on the surface. He reminds his readers that they could drive their cars across most parts of the north of England totally unaware that, literally below their feet, men were working away at the back-breaking task of heaving coal.

Of course, you are only a score of feet below the bridges that cross above you, but the motorists that pound hither and thither across the lanes of Clarke, Heybridge et al are no more aware of your presence than were those of the author of *1984* and, when you finally reach the open air of the viaduct at Bollington and look down on a town-village that seems little changed during the course of a hundred years of photographic record, the feeling of stepping in and out of time is reinforced.

It is now best to speed along the remainder of what becomes an increasingly grannyfied byway and arrive at what was Higher Poynton Station. Here you may require refreshment, not to be found again until The Cheshire Hunt and then only if that is reached in old-fashioned opening hours. The choice is simple: The Boar's Head, which is a pub, and The Coffee Tavern, which isn't. The latter is recorded as serving food in 1866 and, as this was before the railway was completed, it seems we are also travelling along some other and older road.

Once refreshed, take Lyme Road over the canal, bear right at the fork, past Kath's Cattery which is to be congratulated on resisting the obvious temptation with regard to alliterative spelling, and up to the aptly named Windgather House, although the map has the more prosaic Four Winds. This is the edge of Lyme Park and on the skyline you can see the house and pylons of the Bowstones, the next long-term objective.

Lyme Park and Hall have over the centuries been the home of the Legh family and take their name from the term *limites*, meaning boundary, standing as they do on the borders of Cheshire, Lancashire and Derbyshire. The park was renowned for its herd of red deer which, in times past, attracted many visitors, not only to hunt, but also, on every Midsummer's Eve, to watch the unusual and unexplained event of the driving of the herd through the Stag Pond. Dr Richard Pococke in his *Travels Through England* commented that 'it was an extraordinary sight to see their horns like a wood moving through the water.'

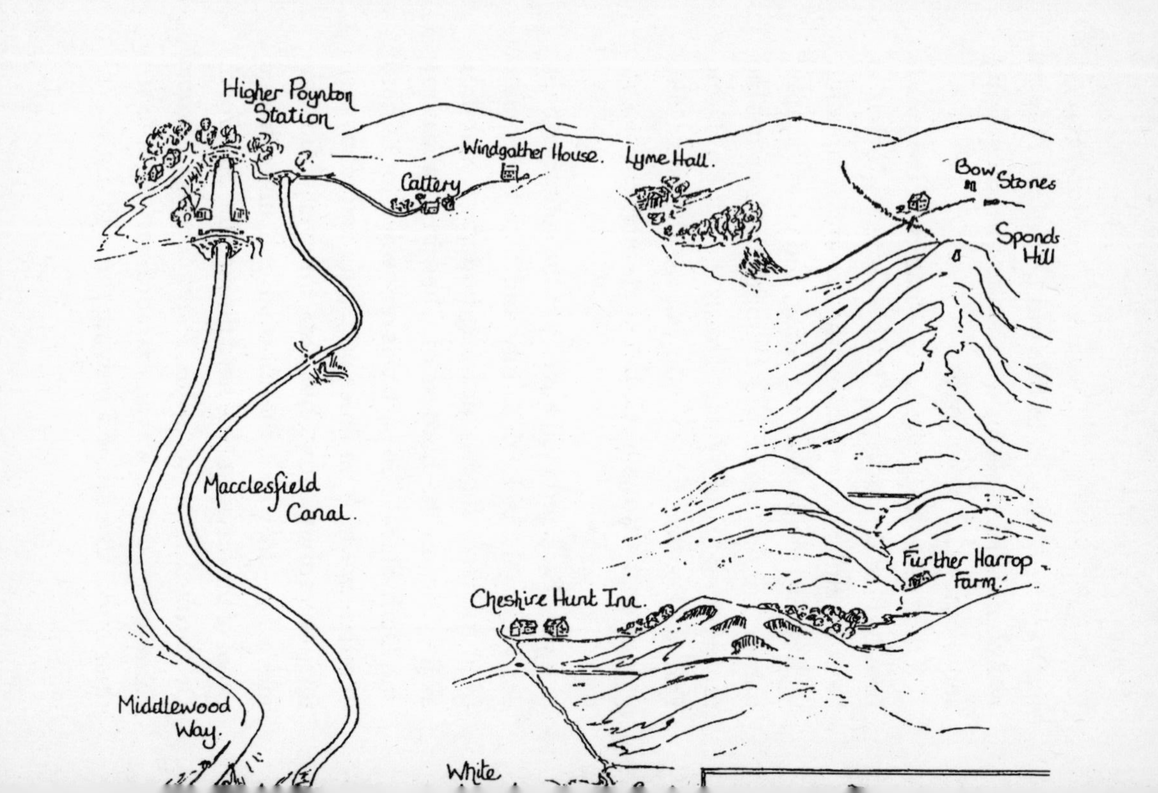

Higher Poynton Station
Windgather House.
Lyme Hall.
Cattery
Bow Stones
Sponds Hill
Macclesfield Canal.
Further Harrop Farm.
Cheshire Hunt Inn.
Middlewood Way.
White

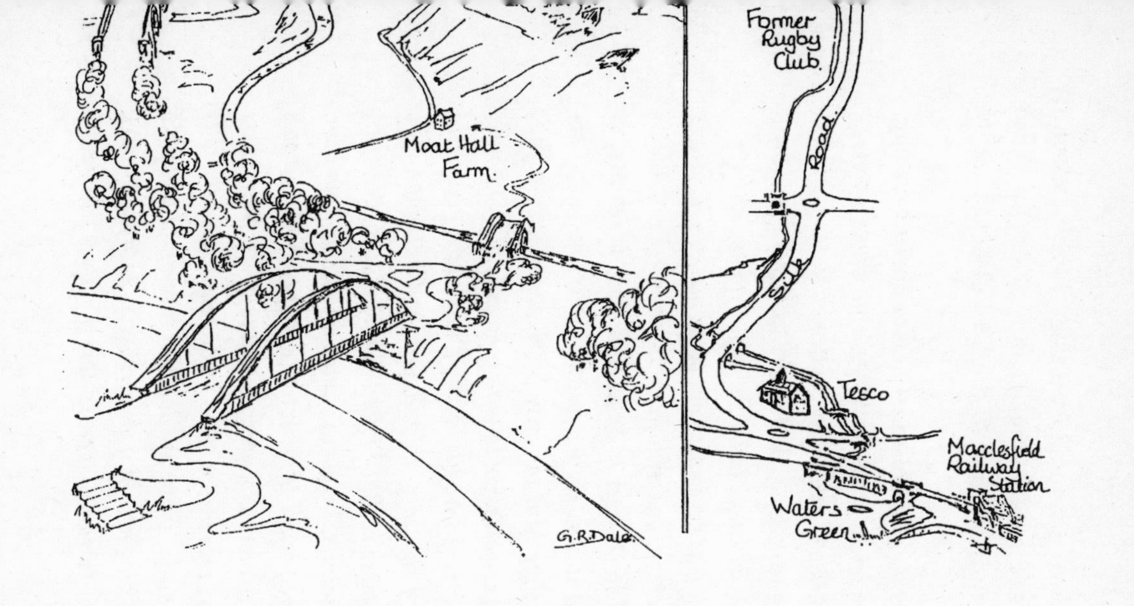

Route One: The Midgrit Trail

However, when hunted, the stags were particularly ferocious, as the following account by Arthur Wilson, a gentleman-in-waiting to the Earl of Essex, shows:

> *Sir Peter Lee of Lime in Cheshire invited my lord one summer to hunt the Stagg. And having a great Stagg in chace, and many gentlemen in the pursuite, the stagg took soyle. And divers (whereof I was one) alighted, & stood with Swords drawne, to have a cut at him, at his coming out of the water. The Staggs there, being wonderful fierce & dangerous, made us youthes more eager to be at him. But he escaped us all. And it was my misfortune to be hindred of my coming nere him the way being sliperie, by a fall. Which gave occasion to some who did not know mee, to speak as if I had falne for feare which being told me, I left the stagg, & followed the Gentleman who (first) spake it. But I found him of that cold temper, that it seemes, his words made an escape from him, as by his denyall & repentance it appeared. But this made me more violent in pursuite of the Stag to recover my reputation. And I happened to be the only horseman in, when the dogs sett him up at a bay; & approaching nere him on horseback, he broke through the dogs, & run at mee, & tore my horse's side with*

his hornes, close by my thigh. Then I quitted my horse, and grew more cunning (for the dogs had sett him up againe) stealing behind him with my Sword, and cut his ham-strings; and then got upon his back & cut his throate. Which as I was doing the Company came in and blamed my rashness, for running such a hazard.

(from Peck's *Desiderata Curiosa*)

The present generation, as the notice on the Westgate entrance suggests, prefers to dispose of them at a somewhat safer range.

Any family with a history as long as the Leghs will inevitably have produced characters of interest. Certainly one fought with distinction at Agincourt, accompanied by his dog, a Lyme mastiff, bred for its 'gigantic head and immensely broad chest'. Perhaps the threat of Shakespeare's Antony to 'Cry havoc, and let slip the dogs of war' was not as metaphorical as we assume. Another equally brave, suspected of anti-Government tendencies, was accused of treason and imprisoned in the Tower.

But it was an employee who probably has the claim to be the most celebrated of them all. Joseph Watson was born in 1648 and appointed Keeper of the Park at the age of twenty-six. He showed extraordinary skill in the job and was reputed to be able to round up and drive the deer as if they were cattle; to amuse his master's guests he would single-handedly drive the herd to the gates of the Hall where it would wait patiently for the visitors' inspection. The ultimate example of this proficiency was demonstrated when, as a result of a wager of 500 guineas between his employer and Sir Roger Mason, he drove twelve brace of stags from Lyme to Windsor Forest as a present to Queen Anne. In his obituary notice it was observed that he drank a gallon of malt liquor a day for sixty years and appears to have stepped up his consumption a notch or two in later life. His drinking habits were of much critical concern to the Legh family and a letter from Sir Peter to Joe's son suggested that the son should step into his father's shoes as it was only a matter of time 'before his old misfortune Friends and Drink' killed him off. This was in 1725. In 1750, at the age of 102, Joe 'hunted a buck a chase for six hours', noting that one of his fellow riders was the great great great grandson of a former hunting companion. It should be mentioned that the disapproving Sir Peter had long since shuffled his mortal coil.

Joe, eventually, died in 1753, having lived through the reigns of seven monarchs, a Protectorate and more than seventy years of marriage.

During this historical digression, the track from Windgather House has led easily through pleasant parkland to the Hall itself. Just before reaching the Hall, there is a signpost marking the Gritstone Trail. Follow this through the wood and up the steepening hillside to the Bowstones and the ridge of Sponds Hill.

At this point, you can look back and forward to see most of what you have done and have yet to do. Although the Stones are of interest as to their origin and purpose, as much is the fact that John Hampson, his wife and three children were buried nearby in 1646. As this was unconsecrated ground, it suggests that they had been socially shunned in some way; it is possible that they died of the Plague which was prevalent at this time. Whatever the reason, the inscription written by Elizabeth Hampson

Think it not strange our bones ly here
Thine may ly thou knowest not where

serves as a reminder of our own fragile grasp of

destiny and the need to guard against passing gratuitous judgment on others.

The walk along the whaleback ridge affords extensive views of most parts of the routes that follow in the first part of this book. Across Chinley to the north-west lies the Kinder Plateau and to the south lies the arc of Shining Tor, Shutlingsloe and Kerridge Ridge. A more detailed identification is available from the viewfinder situated near the path on Sponds Hill itself. The ridge comes to a halt at the road that joins Pott Shrigley to Kettleshulme and the Gritstone Trail, which crosses the higher ground to the right, is temporarily abandoned in favour of a signposted path directly opposite. This descends the fields to Further Harrop Farm, where another signpost indicates a right of way to Harrop Brook. At first the way is not too clear, but a grassy depression deepens into a sunken lane, which in turn links with a footpath that leads through the woods on the banks of the brook and eventually emerges to join Hedge Row, a rough road to civilisation in the shape of the promised Cheshire Hunt. The pub offers an excellent range of real ale and food; there is ample seating outside and the current proprietor is only too happy if you avail yourself of this facility to eat your sandwiches, always providing you make some reciprocal purchase. It was at one time a male-only pub which served the sheep market held in the adjoining field and was known at that time not by its present name but as The Quiet Woman. Today's title suggests a different form of discrimination which, no doubt, will appear to some as equally lacking in Political Exactitude.

The Gritstone Trail is rejoined and is followed tortuously and not obviously round Savio House to the foot of White Nancy. But, with the white monument to guide us, we can cling to the skirts of the trodden way indicated by green splashes on the White Peak Outdoor Leisure Map which show the direction if, at times, conceal the detail. Climb to the monument and follow the ridge to the saddle. At the lowest point a path descends to a road and an entrance to the quarry that has been fenced off to your right. Cross the road and make your way down the driveway to Endon House. Before the buildings are reached, the track turns sharp left and leads back on itself through the woods to a series of stiles that take you over the fields to Moat Hall Farm on Clarke Lane. A signposted track passes the farm and reaches in a few hundred yards a bridge over the canal. Cross the bridge to follow the concessionary path, courtesy of

ICI, and soon will be heard the 'sound of horns and motors' which will bring the traveller to the start of his travail.

Note: Quotations in this chapter relating to Lyme Park are taken from *The House of Lyme*, by Lady Newton.

Two
The Macclesfield Marilyns & the Making of Lists

There is a scene in *Great Expectations* where Pip and Herbert Pocket address the regular problem of their uncertain financial position. To 'order their affairs' Pip draws up a 'Memorandum' of their debts and then comments:

> *When I had all my responsibilities down upon my list, I compared each with the bill and ticked it off. My self-approval when I ticked an entry was quite a luxurious sensation.*

In characteristic fashion, Dickens places a firm finger on not only the dangers but also the pleasures of self-deception. Regardless of worth, making a list gives a sense of order, completing a list a sense of satisfaction.

Mountaineering is not immune from this desire and there is no doubt that since man climbed hills for reasons of recreation rather than labour, he started making lists of what he had done and, more importantly, what he hoped to do. The best known list-maker was Sir Hugh Munro; he and his fellow members of the Scottish Mountaineering Club literally discovered the exact nature of the Highlands of Scotland. Until their exploration, it was generally thought that only some thirty Scottish hills exceeded 3000 feet in height and that Ben Lomond, being the nearest to Glasgow, was the highest, but it was quickly realised that the real figure could be tenfold and that some might well be virgin summits. By 1891 Munro had identified every separate mountain and subsidiary top over 3000 feet and, of course, made a list or, more grandly, a Table. A result of this was to produce a breed or specie of person who collects the separate mountains known as Munros by ascending each in turn, followed by the 'luxurious tick' against the relevant entry. The genus has the usual sub-species: the Common Munroist, whose aim is limited to collecting the 277 separate mountains over 3000 feet; the Lesser Spotted variety who, being afraid of heights, restricts his activities to the Scottish mainland, thus avoiding the spectacular rock scrambling on Skye; and the Greater Backpacked who would only consider the list well and truly ticked when an additional challenge is thrown in, such as completing the table during one journey in reverse alphabetical order. There is also a related cuckoo who loftily dismisses the notion as puerile, yet seems to have a pretty precise idea of how many he has done.

Sad to report, Sir Hugh died before he was able to complete his own list. Although he tried, he failed to climb the (far from) Inaccessible Pinnacle, an inconvenient lump of rock that withstood years of freeze/thaw ravaging to remain thirty feet above its parent mountain, Sgurr Dearg, and the insignificant Carn Cloich-Mhuilinn, which he was saving for his last. Instead, the first person to complete the list of separate mountains was A E Robertson in 1901 who, history records, on reaching the summit of Meall Dearg in Glencoe kissed the cairn and his wife, in that order. The measure of the achievement is that twenty-two years were to pass before the feat was repeated. The second, A R A Burns, like Robertson before him was also a clergyman. Blessed indeed are the listmakers!

With the completion of the list in both senses you would think that would be that. Far from it. Although Munro had made a surprisingly accurate assessment of the heights of his mountains, modern surveying techniques showed the odd error. Hills thought to be over 3000 feet were not and vice versa. Consequently, the Tables had to be revised and this opened the Great Munro Debate. Should the revisers only make changes that reflected more accurate measurement or did they have the remit to make changes in status, relegating former mountains to tops and upgrading their own particular favourites to full Munro status? Like shoppers in the supermarket, they found it hard to resist the temptation of adding the odd attractive morsel to the shopping trolley and, as Dickens suggested, lists have subtler purposes than a mere *aide-memoire.* Changes were made. Mountains that Munro had listed as separate were downgraded, including, ironically, his deliberately saved Carn Cloich-Mhuilinn, and in the latest revision eight new Munros were 'discovered'. Of course, anyone has the right to make any list they choose, but the Revised Version according to St Hamish is not Munro's list and the hills listed can no longer logically be so termed. A possible solution is to name this new set of hills after the quango that begat them: the Scottish Mountaineering All-party Rectification Tribunal formed for the purpose of Altering Lesser Elevations (to) Collectable Status. If this seems a little long-winded, I am sure a suitable acronym could be found.

The fourth ascensionist was J R Corbett who, after completing the Munros, set out to compile a Table of his own. This contained a list of all the mountains in Scotland that lay between the heights of 3000 and 2500 feet. To forestall the bowdlerisation that was to pursue Munro's choice, he stipulated that for a hill to be on his list it must have, in addition to the requisite height, a re-ascent of at least 500 feet on all sides. It would seem, therefore, only re-measurement could alter the status of a Corbett, as they are known, and there could be no debate. Either the mountain was a Corbett or it wasn't. But life is never that simple. It appeared, at one stage, that Corrieyairack Hill and Gairbeinn, both situated just north of the General Wade Road across the Corrieyairrack Pass, were exactly the same height of 896 metres but without the necessary Corbett re-ascent between them. Clearly a Corbett existed. But were they each Corbetts with either being neither? The pragmatist would climb both but find himself in the Kafkaesque position of knowing that he had certainly done something but unsure of what he had actually done. The mountain world held its collective breath on the outcome of this twentieth-century version of the number of angels on the point of a needle controversy. Sad to say, the Ordnance Survey spoiled the party by deciding that Gairbeinn was some four metres higher.

These seminal lists spawned others, the two-thousanders in England and Wales and the two-and-three-quarter-thousanders in Ireland being examples. These jostled for position to equate with Munro status until Alan Dawson produced his list, which seems to have drawn an exact, if somewhat facetious, line. He adopted the Corbett criterion of the 500 feet (150 metre) drop but did not limit himself to a minimum height. Hence he found, to date, in Scotland, England and Wales 1551 points of kurtosis, the technical term for peakedness, which fulfilled his basic ground rule. As you would expect, most of these points correspond to what the average person would consider a hill but there is the odd anomaly. The summit of Bishop Wilton Wold can be surpassed if you travel on a double-decker bus along the A166 and that of Crowborough is a town, but the vast majority, even if lacking in stature, have, by definition, a definition of their own. This list to end all lists sent the mega-bagger wild, kissing cairns and wives (if any remained) in profusion. However, there was a sting in the tail of

Dawson's list. Towards the end of the Scottish section he lists the summits of the St Kilda group. In addition to the highest points of the islands of Hirta, Soay, Dun and Boreray, all of which could be reached with sufficient determination, there are the sea stacks of Stac Lee and Stac an Armin. Although these have been climbed by the likes of Chris Bonington and the Royal Marines, they will stop most mortals in their tracks.

Having made a list, tradition demanded Dawson give it a name. As his list includes most of the Munros and all the Corbetts, eponymity was clearly not only immodest but also inappropriate. So, with Dawson's tongue in Munro's cheek, they were christened Marilyns and this is where Macclesfield comes in. Arguably, within walking distance, there are four Marilyns: Kinder Scout, The Cloud, Gun and Shining Tor. The first three would require transport or a long walk back, but Shining Tor is a convenient high-point of a pleasant round.

The route starts at the wooden bridge and reverses the final section of Route One as far as the saddle on Kerridge Ridge via Moat Hall Farm. If novelty is required, the same point can be reached by continuing along the canal to Clarke Lane, crossing the fields to

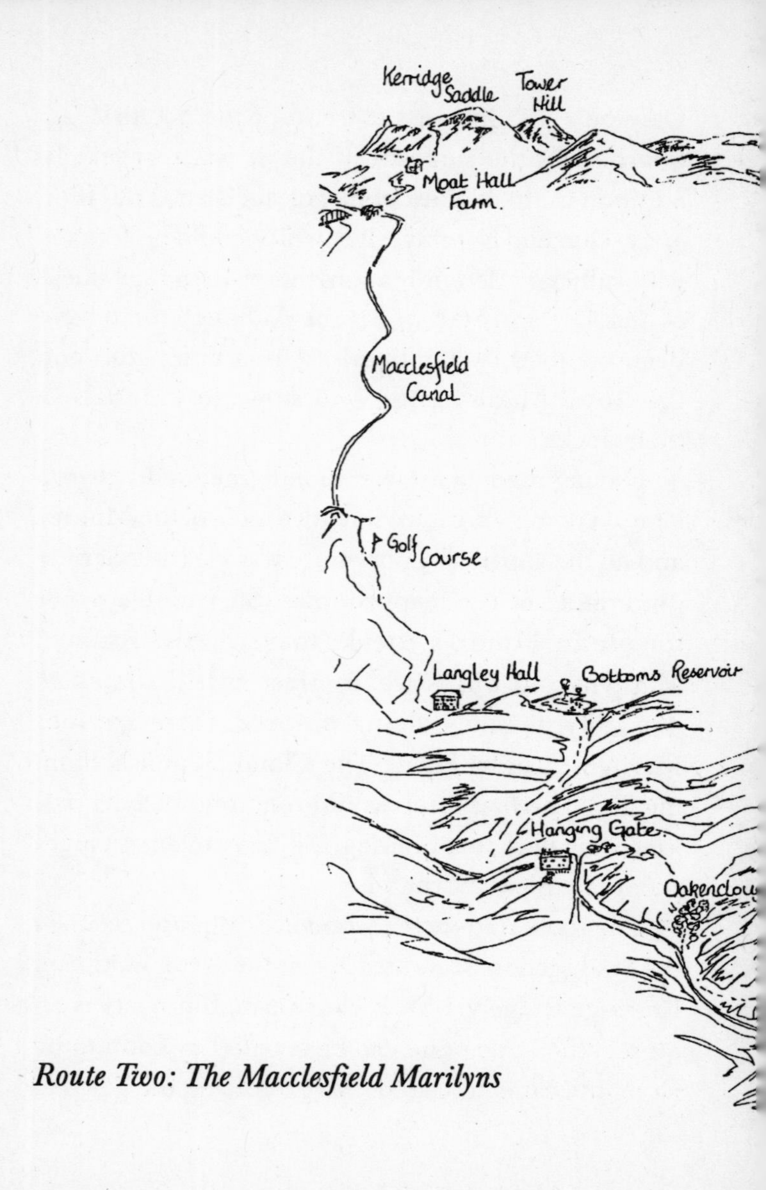

Route Two: The Macclesfield Marilyns

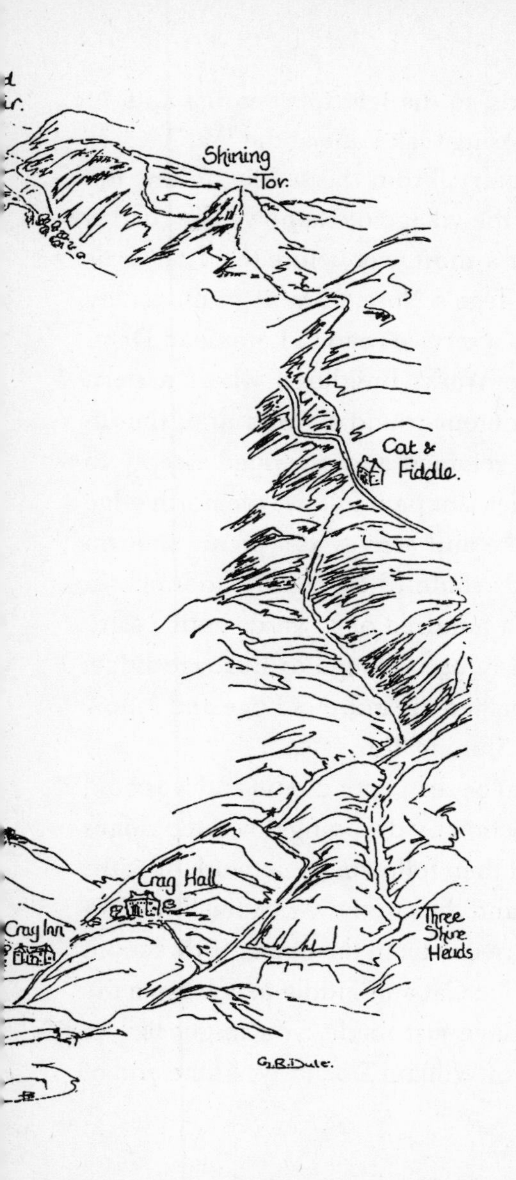
Shining Tor.
Cat & Fiddle.
Crag Hall
Crag Inn
Three Shire Heads
G.B.Dule.

a track which leads, to the left, to a marina and, to the right, after crossing Oak Lane at the War Memorial, to Endon Quarry. From the saddle, follow the Gritstone Trail to the village of Rainow. The road is followed north for a short way before the Trail turns off right towards Tegg's Nose. Almost immediately the lane turns into a service road to Lamaload Dam. Follow this to the Works Buildings, where a stern notice dictates a detour round a wood until the direct route can be rejoined and ascended steeply to the reservoir. A pleasant path follows the north edge of the artificial lake and arrives at a picnic spot on the road that leads south to the A537. Continue in that direction for a hundred or so yards until a signpost signals the way up a clough to Burbage Edge. Climb to the watershed of Andrews Edge and follow it to the Marilyn, Shining Tor.

To the north can be seen Sponds Hill and we could return in that direction by dropping down the ridges to Pym Chair and then following a network of paths to Charles Head and thus to the Gritstone Trail, but there is a more varied walk in the opposite direction. As you set off to The Cat and Fiddle to celebrate the mental tick you have just made, you might like to consider the case of William Docharty. At the end of the First World War, Docharty, serving in France, received a serious leg wound and 'save for a providential collapse on the operating table, should have become a one-legged cripple'. In 1929 he broke his journey from Egypt to Roehampton, where he was to receive further treatment on his leg, at Interlaken and passed the time by taking the train to the viewing point on the Jungfrau Joch. Apart from a short excursion up Ben Lomond, he had no experience of mountaineering, but clearly was struck. He wrote:

> *I had tasted something to which I was not entitled and that crystal atmosphere and virgin snow deserved something better than such casual visitation, the litter of orange peel, banana skins and sandwich paper, or the grinding out of current musical numbers on portable gramophones.*

He pledged that if the Roehampton experiment was successful, he would reach the summit of the Jungfrau on his own feet. It was and he did. He continued to climb in the Alps and extensively in the British Isles and in 1948 completed the Munros and Tops and a year later the 3000 footers 'Furth of Scotland' in England, Wales and Ireland. As his wife's ill health prevented long-distance travel, he concentrated on the British and Irish hills below 3000 feet and in 1954 had privately published his list entitled *A Selection of Some 900 British and Irish Mountain Tops.* This is a meticulous account of mountains and tops for the most part lying between the heights of 3000 and 2500 feet and is a fine edition that contains a slightly apologetic introduction and some outstanding panoramic photographs with, of course, the appropriate technical data. The introduction hints that the job was not complete, nor perhaps ever could be, and eight years later he produced a *Supplement* in two volumes. The primary functions of this edition were to update the 1954 list and then list a selection of a thousand tops under 2500 feet. However, in a preface and an epilogue he released the real man. His recollection of the hills that he had climbed, the trains and boats that had carried him there, the maps that had guided him, the people that he had met and cherished, show that the austerely tabulated lists with their sections and subsections, headings precisely phrased to avoid any ambiguity and the 'carried forward' and 'hereintofore' language of the accountant were only a smokescreen for a very personal and in many ways a private affair, born on a Swiss Alp and consummated during many mountain pilgrimages. He had settled the score of that 'casual visitation'.

However, you should not dally too long as there is still a good way to go. Traverse the moor opposite the pub until you reach the A54 at the foot of Danebower Hollow. Cross the road and, passing a ventilation shaft that serviced Dane Colliery, descend to the River Dane and on to Three Shires Head. Take the track that leads back to the A54, but at Cut-thorn cross fields and the A54 to Crag Hall and drop into Wildboarclough. Follow the road to The Crag Inn, immediately after which field paths take you to Greenaway Bridge and thence to Oakenclough by the stream of the same name. From there a path leads to a walled and muddy lane that arrives at The Hanging Gate, a pub that was originally a toll bar. By crossing the field to the right of the inn, the Gritstone Trail can soon be joined and followed into the village of Langley. (If you wish to shorten the route, you can abandon the moor crossing from The Cat and Fiddle by descending the Cumberland Brook into Wildboarclough and taking the quiet and pleasant road that leads through Macclesfield Forest to the same point.) Pass through the village to Langley Hall, soon after which a path takes you across the Bollin under Birch Knoll and over the Hollins to the Golf Club. You are now once more in Macclesfield and the canal can be picked up to take you to your starting point.

Three
Four Peaks and a Pub Crawl

Peaks? What Peaks, lad? You don't get Peaks in Cheshire! Cheese! That's what you get in Cheshire! Not Peaks! You get Peaks in Yorkshire! Cheshire Cheese. Yorkshire Peaks. That's right, isn't it, Fred? Peaks in Yorkshire. Cheese ...

It is a truth universally acknowledged that one consequence of a pub crawl is that you will receive a sound opinion on most subjects in general and, in addition, the information will, quite selflessly, be repeated several times for your benefit. And it is also true that they do have peaks in Yorkshire. Three to be precise and they are Ingleborough, Penyghent and Whernside and they are called **The Three Peaks**. Despite the efforts of mankind to erode them to the level of the coastal plain by walking, running, cycling and, most probably, wheelbarrow racing around them, they still stand defined as a challenge. You start at Horton-in-Ribblesdale and finish at the same place where, at the café-cum-souvenir-shop, you can buy a badge proclaiming the fact that 'I have bagged The Three Peaks', which completes the set of 'I have walked the Pennine Way' and 'I have climbed Snowdon with my friend Tracey'. This Human Race can obliterate the landscape to such an extent that, on a cloudy day, interest can be reduced to avoiding falling down Hunt Pot or admiring the skills of the engineers who built the railway viaduct at Ribblehead.

The excitement that the latter, from time to time, induces is a good example of the selfish sentimentalism that so often pervades the issue of conservation. The viaduct is showing its age; to repair it would be very expensive. The bureaucratic answer is to close the line between Settle and Carlisle. This, however, brings wails of horror from Middle Englanders who rush to the aid of the man and his dog who would be seriously inconvenienced if this were to happen. Bureaucracy responds to Government pressure not to endanger its prospects at the next election. Another coat of structurally supporting whitewash is applied to the bridge and the self-righteous return to their travels to and from Carlisle by roaring up and down the M6 in their BMWs. If you really want to save something, you must use it, whether it is a rail service or the local Post Office, not when it suits your convenience or in a moment of 'What shall we do this weekend, darling?' 'Oh, I don't know - let's save a bridge', but when it is less than convenient and as a matter of principle.

There is another Three Peaks race which was quite popular forty years ago. The idea was to ascend the highest summits in Wales (Snowdon), England (Scafell) and Scotland (Ben Nevis) within twenty-four hours. As there were no such things as motorways and most roads north of Glasgow were single-tracked, the feat was in the driving rather than the climbing and the challenge nowadays has rather lost its point. Whether you could do it by train within the time limit would be quite interesting, though I suppose the Welsh element would be rather too easy. The best way is to sail.

The idea of a walk joining a number of pubs is also traditional. Perhaps the most notorious is The Four Inns Walk that connects outlying points in the Peak District. It became a training exercise for such activities as The Duke of Edinburgh's Award and the crossing became an annual event. In 1964 three scouts lost their way in a blizzard on Bleaklow and died before the search parties, themselves hampered by atrocious conditions, could reach them. There is a danger inherent in Virtual Reality.

Although Macclesfield might not have 'Three Peaks', it does have on its doorstep four interesting and varied Hills and, to tip the balance, the suggested walk has six Inns. The four hills form the staggered wave that overlooks the town and from north to south are Kerridge Hill, Tegg's Nose, Shutlingsloe and Croker Hill. The Inns are The Rising Sun, The Leathers Smithy, The Crag Inn, The Hanging Gate, The Ryles Arms and The Fool's Nook, which, if care is not taken, can form a wavering stagger. If a challenge is required, half a pint of whatever you deem prudent in each within the traditional opening hours of 11.00 to 3.00, in addition to reaching the summits of the Macclesfield Four, would require you to stretch your legs. The sporting could start at The Bull in Kerridge and make a direct assault on White Nancy.

Make your now familiar way on to the Kerridge Ridge and follow that to the south end, where the trig point is situated. Retrace your steps and follow paths that pick up the Gritstone Trail and, after passing the remains of a water mill, follow a lane to reach the B5470. The Rising Sun is a little way up on your right. This is the only time you don't pass the front door of one of the inns on your circuit. The route turns left and continues along the road until you reach Berristall Lane. Instead of following the road to Lamaload, bear half-right once you have passed the cottages and take a path that leads up towards a wooded area. As you rise above Rainow, the Trail keeps pleasantly to the high ground until it falls towards a farm track. Here turn sharp right and, after entering the second field, drop to a small bridge that crosses a brook and climb steeply to the A537, the 'new' road from Macclesfield to Buxton. Cross the road (carefully) and enter the fields beyond through a gate. These lead to the 'old' road at Windyway House, with the Tegg's Nose car-park a little further to your right.

Assuming speed is not of the essence, you can spend some time in this area designated as a Country Park. Refreshment is available, together with a good deal of information on the surrounding landscape. There is a good viewpoint, but the most interesting aspect is an open-air quarry museum where you can inspect the various ponderous pieces of machinery used for crushing, sawing and shifting stone. Whatever you do, you must pick a path that leads to the summit of Tegg's Nose. Do not be too encouraged by the sign that reads Croker Hill 8.1km; this does not assume that you will have to turn sharp left to take in Shutlingsloe. Descend from the summit on a wide and obvious path which leads to Tegg's Nose Reservoir. Cross the dam to the road and follow it alongside Bottoms Reservoir. Instead of taking the signposted Trail, continue a few hundred yards to the largest of the reservoirs, Ridgegate, on the corner of which will be found The Leathers Smithy. Two down - two to go.

To tackle Shutlingsloe, which is arguably the finest hill in the district and from certain angles deserves its sobriquet The Matterhorn of the Peak, continue along the road to the highest of the reservoirs, Trentabank. This secluded water surrounded by the woods of Macclesfield Forest is inhabited by a variety of wildfowl; of particular interest are the goldeneye and occasional goosander. At the information centre opposite, a clear path leads through the trees on to a shoulder and up the final slopes to the peaky summit. Due west lies The Hanging Gate and re-entry to the Gritstone Trail but the only official line of access, other than retracing our steps, is south-east into Wildboarclough. This means we have to descend to The Crag Inn and follow the route across the fields to Oakenclough, described in the second chapter.

It is always annoying to move in an opposite line to your general direction of travel and the subject of Access to Open Countryside has caused its fair share of controversy on the jealously guarded grouse moors of the Peak. The trouble is that the debate tends to be polemic, with 'Property is theft' on the one hand and 'How would you like me to take *my* family for a picnic in *your* front garden?' on the other. As both these arguments are quite easy to sustain, the discussion tends to generate more heat than light. In fact they are not mutually incompatible but deal with separate issues: *(a)* the right to use land for profit or pleasure and *(b)* the right to privacy and security.

Forbidding access is not the only way to secure the second objective. In some countries there is unlimited access to open country but it is an offence for anyone, without a proper reason, to encroach within a certain distance (usually 150m) of inhabited dwellings and farm buildings. The area that this enclosed would be 'owned' in the sense that we understand the term and would place the dweller in the country on the same footing as his counterpart in the town. This would ensure privacy and security, yet allow the public to enjoy the benefits of the open air. Indeed, the 'Neighbourhood Watch' of law-abiding walkers and climbers could well discourage vandalism and theft and, as such, offset any damage caused by unclosed gates.

The question of land use is more vexed. The present system of land tenure introduced by the Normans was invented to control a country that had no easy means of communication. The King gave Yorkshire to Lord X in return for reciprocal favours such as keeping the natives from revolting. Lord X, after keeping the better parts for himself, sub-divided the county on the same conditions. If Lord X or any of his subordinates stepped out of line, they lost the right to use the land and the King took it back. This also fitted in neatly with contemporary philosophical thinking - that all life was a chain with God at the top and all matter below in a proper, descending order. It went something like: God, King of England, Posh Englishmen, Ordinary Englishmen, the rest of Europe, women, and so on to the sticks and stones at the tail. The captive peasant was told every Sunday that it was God's idea that His Lordship should live in a mansion whilst he and several others lived in a hovel. Poverty was to be seen as a long-term endowment policy and being rich wasn't all it was cracked up to be - in fact, it was jolly hard work.

Given that this might appear a little outmoded as we approach the next millennium, perhaps the structure could be altered. If we started from the premise that, save for 'owned' buildings as previously defined, all land was common property, then individuals could apply for use for such purposes as farmland or grouse moor. In return for the licence to do this, they would have to agree to an appropriate level of access. I agree it sounds awkward and bureaucratic but merely because the present system is easy to administer does not make it right.

The concomitant of this would be for the public to accept that the concept of Right of Way is equally outdated. Many of these existed for reasons long since forgotten and to insist that the world and his wife can march through someone else's back garden because a postman from Time Immemorial has had to take this route to deliver a letter to a neighbouring farm is as equally unreasonable as it is for us to be denied the right to walk in a straight line across rough country direct from the summit of Shutlingsloe to the hospitality of The Hanging Gate.

Even if this solution is flawed, it at least attempts the compromise that must be sought if we are to avoid confrontation and unpleasantness. Too often heads go in the sand. A good example of this is Sir Hugh Munro, himself a landowner who, needing to invade the property of others to complete his list, would on

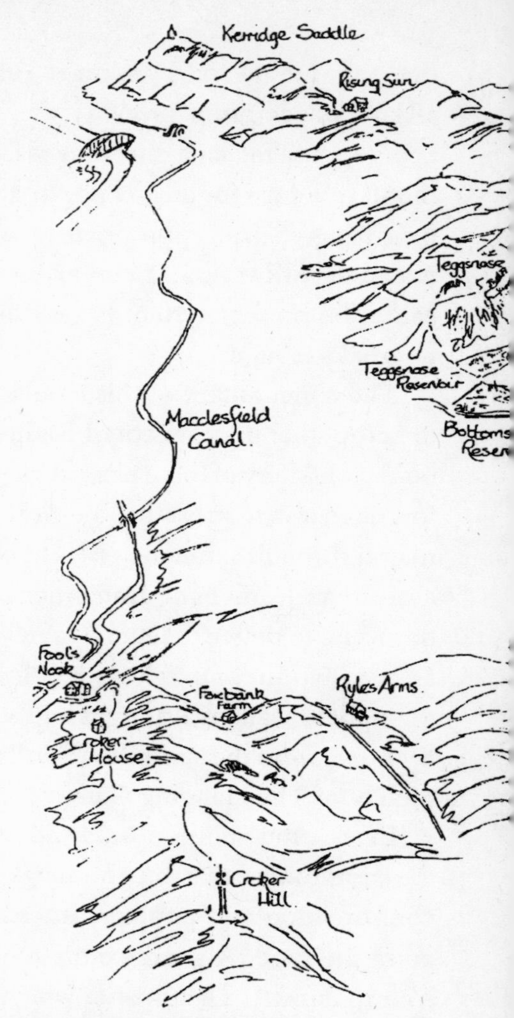

Route Three: Four Peaks & a Pub Crawl

Smithy
Trentabank
Reservoir
Macclesfield.
Forest.
Shutlingsloe
Oakenclough
Crag Inn

occasion make his entry and exit under the cover of darkness. It is this kind of double standard that lies at the heart of the problem.

Leave the Hanging Gate and cross the field to join the Gritstone Trail just below Fernlee. The yellow markers are not in such profusion here, but you can't go wrong if you keep heading for the Radio Tower on Croker Hill. You cross a stile with a footprint on the step; keep high above Rossendale Brook until another is reached, this time in a wall. Descend the field to the left corner where a bypass enables you to reach the rear car-park of The Ryles Arms. The Trail proper, which seems to have a strong Temperance streak, avoids this temptation and follows the brook to Lowerhouse. If you divert for refreshment, you will have to walk a few hundred yards down the road to reach the same place. A signpost points the way past Foxbank Farm and the path goes directly up on to the ridge of Sutton Common, which leads to Croker Hill. On a clear day the outlook is rewarding and acts as a counterpoint to the view described from Sponds Hill. To the west is the Cheshire Plain; to the north and east the route covered during the day, with the Buxton Moors as a backdrop, and to the south the continuing Trail to Mow Cop and the start of the

Staffordshire Way. Retrace your steps until you reach a track leading down to a farm on your left. Pass the farm and Croker House (now a catotel to balance Kath's Lyme Park enterprise). The track turns into the metalled road of Croker Lane. At the junction turn left on to the old Leek Road and follow it down to the new main road and the canal, with its automatic swing bridge. The Fool's Nook will soon be reached. If you are interested in the origins of this unusual name the landlord will supply an explanatory pamphlet on request.

Now that you have reached the sixth inn of the day, it might be worth considering the part such establishments have played in the history of walking and climbing. All recognised centres had their own pub. In North Wales the Pen-y-Gwyrd, with its Everest autographed ceiling, catered for the old school and the Padarn Lake in Llanberis for the new. Similarly, climbers in the Lake District adopted hotels which, in time, became the unofficial headquarters of the Fell & Rock Climbing Club - The Sun Inn in Coniston, The Old Dungeon Ghyll in Langdale and, most famously, The Wastwater Hotel under the slopes of Gable, Scafell and Pillar. Scotland, with its vaster distances, does not generally allow the same clubby atmosphere, although The King's House and The Clachaig at each end of Glencoe have been treated in this manner by generations of climbers. More often, they are the only outposts of civilisation or, in bad conditions, a refuge to which the walker can turn. Like petrol stations in the Highlands, it's always best to fill up when you see one. The interaction of hotel and climber is well illustrated by the following encounter described by W H Murray in his classic work *Mountaineering in Scotland*:

> *I amused myself by reminding Dunn of the less creditable episodes of his climbing career. He is one of the most hopelessly casual and yet friendly of men. To cite but one incident, typical of his way of life, he once sent me a telegram from the wilds of Kintyre, commanding me to climb with him on Nevis next day - but omitting to state time or place of meeting. I set off by car from Glasgow, staking all upon a chance encounter somewhere in Lochaber. Half-way there, I happened to stop at Inverarnan hotel in Glen Falloch - to find Dunn, large and fair-haired, sprawling before the fire and wolfing hot scones and tea. I advanced to unleash my thunder, when 'Good man!' cried Dunn, 'I knew it was two to one you'd stop at*

Inverarnan.' You cannot damn and blast a man whose eye is sparkling with delight at meeting you. I tried; but it was no use.

There are, of course, pubs and pubs and, as Katherine Hopkinson in her contribution to the 1922 Fell & Rock Journal states, 'There are in the Lake District two perfectly distinct classes of hotel: (1) The hotel which is really an inn; (2) The hotel proper which is an anathema.' For most, the inn at Wasdale will represent the first type most completely. Hopkinson again, now in a lyrical but, I fear, potentially elegiac mood:

> *Soon after the Styhead footpath reaches the green valley divided by thick stone walls into squares and triangles of pasturage, it is joined from the right by a narrow lane. Where this lane enters the main road to the coast, past the miniature, whitewashed church in its little enclosure planted with yew trees, stands another whitewashed building, long and low, at right angles to a big, grey stone barn and backed by the stream which tumbles down from Black Sail. It is the Wasdale Head Hotel, the Mecca of climbing-men. In the hall are rows of tremendous hobnailed boots*

and rubber climbing shoes. A couple of ropes are coiled about the baluster knob. There are ice-axes in the umbrella stand and an elusive odour of dubbin and wet tweed pervades the atmosphere. The coffee-room is of the old and gregarious type with one long table running down the centre of the room. Round the walls hang photographs of great climbs and renowned climbers, including one specially fine enlargement of Will Ritson, the celebrated landlord who reigned in Wasdale a generation ago.

If this sounds all rather cosy and civilised, it should be balanced by events in the billiard room. In his recollections of rock climbing in the Lake District, Bentley Beetham, a stalwart of the club who did much to open up the less fashionable nooks and crannies of the area, recalls a less decorous image of the 'gregarious' activities:

The best and most strenuous of all was Wasdale Fives. What Homeric struggles have been staged around that ancient table! Many legends exist about that strange game, and for the benefit of those who knew it not, it may be added that it was played with a billiard ball and the naked hand as a striker. It was for two or four players. The server slung the ball against the top cushion so that on its return it touched the top left one. The man served to stood near the bottom left pocket, and he had to prevent the ball reaching the bottom cushion, otherwise a point was scored by the server. If the service was returned, as it usually was, the ball was in play and could be struck by anyone on either side alternately, a point being won if you put the ball into the top left pocket, made it rebound from the top cushion to the bottom one, or if the ball after being struck by your side, ceased to roll before an opponent reached it.... Those who had played most British games and a few exotics besides, generally agreed that none demanded more energy, activity and initiative or provided better sport and excitement than Wasdale Fives. Occasionally tourist visitors to the inn might be attracted by the noise and innocently look in to see what was going on. The door was near the top end of the table, the danger zone, and before they knew what was happening, an ivory billiard ball might come hurtling through the air towards them to crash into the boarding at their side. They seldom stayed long at that end of the room.'

(Fell & Rock Climbing Club Journal, 1942)

It is a pity that nowadays most people's idea of a country pub is a plastic dinosaur in the children's play area and a microwaved Sunday lunch at 'Unbeatable Prices', and that a country walk is along the ever-deepening mudbath of a 'concessionary' access.

But the walk is over and you must leave The Fool's Nook and return to Macclesfield. You may have made arrangements to be taxied, either commercially or uxoriously. If not, you will have to take to the tow-path and hope you can thumb a lift from some passing barge.

Four
The Macclesfield-Edale
or **A Clutch of Cartographers**

Near the start of his novella, *Heart of Darkness*, Conrad has his narrator explain what prompted his interest in travel:

> *Now when I was a little chap I had a passion for maps. I would look for hours at South America, or Africa, or Australia, and lose myself in the glories of exploration. At that time there were many blank spaces on the earth and when I saw one that looked particularly inviting on a map I would put a finger on it and say, When I grow up I will go there.*

The Macclesfield-Edale route is part of such a concept, rather than a journey in its own right. Imagine a map of England which is blank apart from a meandering line starting at Berwick-on-Tweed and finishing at Land's End. You can call this line 'The All England Way' but you won't find it in any guidebook or on any published map because you have just drawn it yourself. Such a line *might* follow the Scottish border to the watershed between the North and Irish Seas, swing south down the Pennines with possibly a zig into the Howgills and a zag into the Yorkshire Dales, then leave the north via the Gritstone and Staffordshire Trails. This would place it in canal country and it could follow the towpath towards Llangollen and the Way of Offa, and continue south through the Marches to link up with the softer uplands of Cotswold, Mendip and Quantock before tackling the more testing moors and coastpaths of Devon and Cornwall to finish at Dr Syntax's Head and England's Toe.

It might follow this line but it probably will not, as the point of the idea is that you design the route to suit your own purposes. There is no need to do it in a single journey; you could do it a bit at a time. However, it would be, in the main, more satisfactory if you started at one end and returned to the place where you had previously stopped, rather than attacking it piecemeal. A short section could be adjacent to a nearby holiday (Long Distance Walking without pain) or a whole section could be swallowed in a determined week under canvas. You could adopt as a theme a literary pilgrimage, a visit to all Football League Clubs beginning with M, or even a rather elaborate way of fulfilling the promise to all those friends and relatives that you would 'drop in on, one day'.

Unlike Conrad's hero, most people's domestic and occupational commitments mean that they have a limited number of choices as to how they use their free time. The extremes are either to attempt to skate across the greatest range of experience or to concentrate on the detail of a limited area. This chapter favours the latter and puts forward the proposition that a thorough knowledge of your own country provides a satisfaction that a superficial understanding of others will not give. There are additional advantages: England has better maps than average and the natives, for the most part, speak English.

If you want to get an idea of the extreme possibilities involved in such a scheme, you might like to look at Dave Hewitt's book, *Walking the Watershed*, which describes a journey from the Scottish Border to Cape Wrath, keeping to the highest ground at all times. As with all watershed walks, there are times when you feel you are walking round in circles. Your night's destination is within spitting distance but you are yanked by the collar to circumnavigate an enormous corrie that houses an ineffectual but critical trickle of water. The bare statistics are 850 miles of walking, 100,000 metres of ascent and a time of eighty days. Further comment seems superfluous.

This demonstrates a particular determination embraced by only the few, so for the many the casual meander is encouraged. Not least because it will give you an excuse to buy certain OS maps that otherwise you might regard as an indulgence. I would prefer to own a set of such maps from 1-203 rather than a set of the Encyclopaedia Britannica or even the complete OED, but I would find it difficult to justify the purchase of, for example, map 139 unless it were to find the quickest way out of Birmingham. However, if you are trying to link together the more obvious hilly areas of the country, you will need to examine in some detail maps that otherwise you might not open.

Such a link is the subject of this chapter. There is no problem finding a variety of ways from Northumberland to Edale and from Macclesfield into the canal systems. The route described fills the gap. To conform to the pattern, it is described from south to north. You leave the Netherland Bridge and gain the

Gritstone Trail which is followed to the Bowstones. This is the reverse of the end of Route One, with the exception that, rather than following the valley of Harrop Brook, it crosses it by a packhorse bridge and continues across fields under Andrew's Knob to Brink Farm. A short distance along the road Route One is rejoined. From the Bowstones, drop down the road to The Moorside Hotel. From here there are alternatives. Either keep to the paths that traverse the high ground of Whaley Moor or follow a track that passes through Cliff. Whichever you choose, you will eventually be driven on to lanes or roads that lead down to Whaley Bridge. The advantage of the Cliff track is that it runs into a lane that has twisted its way from Kettleshulme across a stream at Kishfield Bridge. Continue down the lane until you pass Toddbank Farm which lies a little below you on your right. The next property is Croft Cottage. A path passes between it and a telegraph pole and drops down to Toddbrook Reservoir, where the imaginatively named Reservoir Road leads to Whaley Bridge. It is not signposted and is easily missed. But it does not really matter as there is another attractive public footpath a little further on which leads to the same place. This is set back on the right. It is worthwhile picking up one of these paths as it enables you to visit a well-tended pond which is situated just below the dam. Whatever happens, you will eventually fall into the railway station and the Arms of Jodrell.

Whaley Bridge has a sufficient cluster of pubs to challenge Macclesfield in the contiguity stakes but it is best to resist temptation and push on to Buxworth. In keeping with the general philosophy, I can offer at least three ways. There are green paths to the right; these cross the *Roosdyche*, the particular shape of which romantic history had as a Roman racecourse but modern science corrects to the much more interesting concept of a glacial overflow channel. There is the High Peak Canal to the left and the chosen route in the centre. This Media Via crosses the A5004 and continues down a side street past the Goyt Inn until a signpost is picked up directing the walker along the Goyt, then up to join Bings Road which leads through Gnat Hole to Buxworth, or Bugsworth as it was known until the town worthies had the name changed in 1934. This involves a good bit of road work, but the lane is generally quiet and the profusion of flora and fauna contrasts favourably with the nondescript moorland silence that is too often the lot of the walker in the Peak. The choice is further justified when you discover that you are descending Silk Hill, a reference to the fact that you are walking on the old packhorse road that led to Macclesfield. More echoes.

Whichever way you choose, you will have to pass The Navigation Inn, which is open all day, every day. CAMRA describes it as an 'excellent, multi-roomed pub with an extensive restaurant alongside the only remaining UK canal tramway'. The notice on the door describes it as 'probably the best pub in the world'. It *is* good. Real ale, real food and real fires. Bargepainted decor. Interesting memorabilia - there are two out of six remaining wheels from the mineral wagons used on this line, the other four are in the York Railway Museum. Worth stopping as it must be near lunchtime.

Continuing through Buxworth, you wonder why they went to such lengths to change the name. As it was, the refined would have pronounced it Begsworth and the vulgar will still dwell on the 'u' to the extent that the following consonant will be indistinguishable from the original. It must all be a question of headed notepaper. Pass under the railway, take a lane and paths across fields via Cotebank to reach Over Hill Road. A right and left turn picks up tracks that skirt Chinley Churn and lead past Hills Farm to run

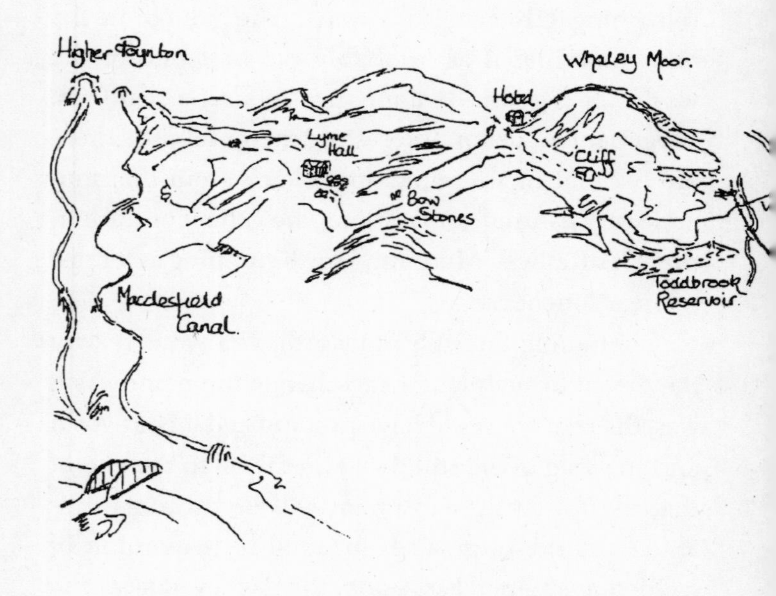

Route Four: Macclesfield-Edale

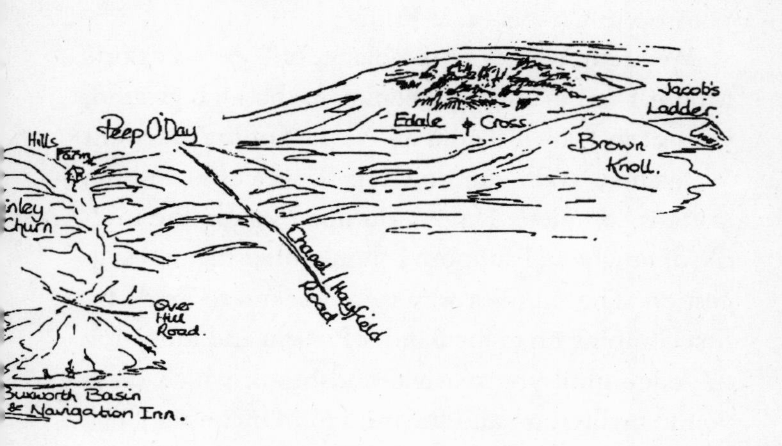
Jacob's Ladder.
Edale Cross.
Brown Knoll.
Peep O'Day
Hills Farm
inley Churn
Chapel Road.
Hayfield
Over Hill Road.
Buxworth Basin & Navigation Inn.

down to Peep o' Day on the A624 that connects Glossop to Chapel-en-le-Frith.

We are now back to the black stuff. A track skirts Mount Famine and, by keeping to the high ground, you reach Brown Knoll, an outpost of the Derwent Watershed. Walls run down to Edale Cross and the route is complete. Having dumped you in the middle of nowhere, I suppose I should offer the odd suggestion. The simplest way is to descend to Edale by first climbing on to the Kinder Plateau and following the edge until you reach Grindsbrook which takes you to civilisation and the train to Manchester. (The reader may punctuate this last statement as he thinks fit.) If time permits, rather than turn right, you could continue to Kinder Low and walk clockwise round the rim until the ridge of Ringing Roger (originally Rocher) can be descended to the same place.

Whilst in this area, the ghost of Conrad may well reappear. During his trip to Africa Marlow observes at first hand the enlightened effect of civilisation on the locals. At one point, he passes a file of emaciated natives, chained together, eyes fixed to the ground and carrying excessively heavy loads. If you should come across such a group toiling up Jacob's Ladder, don't be alarmed. It is not an extreme measure to move sections of the population from Welfare to Work, merely the latest batch of Penninewayers who are ejected from The Nag's Head at regular intervals to begin their pilgrimage to the Church at Yetholm.

The squeamish, to avoid this display of post Neo-Thatcherism, should turn south at Brown Knoll and work their way back to the safer waters of Goyt and Langley via Coombes Moss. But, whatever you do, you will need a map and this chapter is meant to celebrate not only the explorers but also the map-makers. Docharty again, in similar vein to Conrad:

> *Since the days when my father so enthusiastically explained to me as a tiny boy the interest, beauty and vast store of information to be found upon good maps and taught me how to read them, these beautiful works of compound effort, and essential companions of all who leave the beaten track, have afforded me the utmost pleasure.*

Of all the devices that the OS have thought up to get us around, the invention of contours must be high in the list of honours. This came about as a by-product of a more ambitious project. In 1774 one Maskelyne decided to put into practice Isaac Newton's theory that if you could measure the swing of a plumb line towards a suitably symmetrical mountain and you could measure the weight of the mountain, you could calculate the weight of the Earth. There were, of course, at this time no maps. Schiehallion, on the edge of Rannoch Moor, was discovered and thought to fit the bill. It was conical, of consistent mass and sufficiently isolated from neighbouring gravitational forces. As part of the process of finding out how much Schiehallion weighed, the Astronomer Royal employed the Army to place chains round the mountain to join points of equal height. One of the surveyors, Hutton, realised the potential of these less than imaginary lines and contours were born.

I can claim a minor footnote in the history of this experiment. It was during one Easter that I was climbing in the area with a friend who taught Physics at a Sixth Form College. Ron had an inventive turn of mind and thought that a suitable selection of slides demonstrating Maskelyne's experiment would enliven the teaching of scientific principles to his not particularly strong set of A Level students. I was despatched to various points on the skyline to illustrate the engineering problems involved, photographed holding pieces of rock to demonstrate the consistent density of the hill and eventually swinging an ice-axe in the manner of the plumb line. All these visual aids were duly shown with appropriate explanations to the class. When summer approached and revision was in full flow, Ron asked if there were any areas they would like to go over. To his surprise, he received the first response in two years from a pupil who had up to that point sat impassively throughout the course, staring out of the window.

'Of course, James. What would you particularly like me to do?'

'Do you think there's any chance we could see your holiday slides again, sir?'

Five
A 'Lang Stride' or A Walk with Interludes

This walk, which is the final one in the Macclesfield section, does not cover that much in the way of new ground, but rather throws a cordon around the area to form a challenging long distance walk. Nevertheless, it has some interesting passages and, as such, can be regarded as a yardstick by which to judge your stamina and determination before undertaking the better known walks of a similar nature which are found throughout Britain. Three examples of these are to be examined in Part Two. It ought to be mentioned in passing that these are of a different order from the Macclesfield excursions and require more than rudimentary navigational skills and, on occasion, the confidence to move easily and quickly over exposed and technical rock ridges.

It is traditional in estimating the time required to cross rough and mountainous terrain to apply Naismith's Rule. This states that you should allow one hour for every three miles on the ground and half an hour for every thousand feet of ascent. This does not take into account any rest taken or load carried. As the distance of this walk is approximately fifty-five miles and it has its share of ups and downs, it is clear that it cannot be walked according to Naismith within the course of a typical day's outing. The approved method for 'walks' of this length is to run all the flat and downhill and rest while walking uphill as briskly as possible. In my experience, if this is sustained over eight to ten hours, you can comfortably average five miles an hour in the Peak District, four miles an hour in the Lakes or North Wales and three miles an hour in the rough terrain of the Scottish Highlands. This is regardless of ascent. If the course lasts longer than half a day, other factors come into play. Dehydration, which can be avoided, and darkness, which can't, are the obvious examples. By applying this revised formula, you should allow eleven hours to complete the round. The only alternative for those who feel seriously threatened by having both feet simultaneously off the ground is to do it in two parts. In any event, it would be best to check the lie of the land before making a continuous attempt.

We will start by appeasing the various powers of darkness that we might encounter and do it clockwise rather than withershins. This means once more making the trek along the Gritstone Trail to Sponds Hill. At this point there is some way still to go but the advancing in years can take heart from the dictum of Dick Crawshaw who felt that serious long distance walking could only be undertaken by those approaching middle age. To underline the point he broke the non-stop walk record in 1974 at the age of fifty-four. He exceeded 250 miles in just over seventy-six hours, a distance that was thought, at the time, to be the limit of human endurance. From Sponds Hill you have only forty-five or so left, a mere bagatelle.

Continue along the ridge but do not go as far as Bowstones. Instead turn right on to a waymarked path that falls to the junction of Higher and Holehouse Lanes. Take the latter, which links Kettleshulme to Whaley Bridge (see Route Four), and follow it down to Kishfield Bridge. At the bridge you will see a stile and a memorial sign that points the way to Gap House and Taxal. Cross the stile and follow as best you can the sunk rather than sunken lane that leads past some farm buildings and Gap House to the Macclesfield-Whaley Bridge Road, the B5470. Cross the major road, avoid the minor version and take the minimus up left to a disused quarry. This leads via lanes or footpaths to Taxal itself. Walk through the hamlet and after 200 yards cut across an open area where a signposted path leads down to the River Goyt, which is followed into the reservoired valley. A better, if more convoluted, option is to ascend Taxal Edge and then cut down to the valley via a variety of paths. However, the whole area is under access review and a preliminary reconnoitre is recommended.

The history of the development of this area is revealing. One assumes from time immemorial there has been farming in the vicinity but it probably kept well clear of the Chilworth Gunpowder Factory situated in the valley itself. This supplied the wherewithal to thwart the Armada - a sort of sixteenth-century Sellafield. The Victorians brought in a paint factory (another whitewash?), cottages for twenty employees and their families, a railway to carry limestone to Whaley Bridge, and Errwood Hall built by Samuel Grimshaw. This community spawned the usual paraphernalia, a school, burial ground and a coal mine to feed the open fires of Errwood. However, the middle of the twentieth century demanded more and more water and after the death of the last member of the Grimshaw family in 1930, Stockport Corporation was able to buy the estate. In 1937 the north end of the valley was flooded to create Fernilee and in 1968 the Duchess of Kent oversaw the submergence of the rest when Errwood Reservoir was created. The Hall itself, after a short period as a Youth Hostel, was demolished because of the danger of pollution and an uneasy truce broke out between the landscape that had been gardened and the natural moorland habitat. I suppose each 'improvement' was deemed to have 'ruined' the existing state of affairs. Photographs taken before the flooding do indeed appear idyllic but the current combination of moor, trees and water is arguably just as attractive and it is, perhaps, worth remembering that evidence of the past tends to be somewhat selective.

When you reach the dam of Fernilee, pick up the dismantled railway track (an interesting metaphysical concept) and make good speed to Errwood. At the dam follow the road uphill until a path can be found that goes behind the Sailing Club and crosses through fields and woods to the foot of the Wild Moor where Wildmoorstone Brook joins the reservoir. A path follows the brook to rejoin the railway at a blocked tunnel. Climb past the tunnel to reach

Burbage Edge. Follow the Edge and a series of paths to reach the main Macclesfield-Buxton Road. In doing this, you will have crossed the old road that leads down to Derbyshire Bridge and are probably following the route of the salt smugglers who would choose this inhospitable terrain to avoid paying tax. A path leads on to Axe Edge Moor and, as far as Macclesfield is concerned, you are on the edge of all things.

To someone who has lived a substantial portion of his life in the North East of England the idea that we are now standing on a coalfield is somewhat incongruous. Records show that the Duke of Devonshire mined extensively in the area, although I imagine he got some other chaps to do the tricky bits, and, in fact, there were about 130 pits at the Axe Edge and Thatch Marsh workings. This is not quite what it sounds, as a pit meant any incursion into the seam. At the start the coal would be mined at the point of outcrop, open cast, as it were. Then, when that became impracticable, a shaft would be sunk and the coal raised up that by hand. As the seam went deeper into the ground, further shafts, now worked by horse engine, would be employed. The reason for all this activity was to provide coal which, though of a low grade, was sufficient to burn the locally quarried lime essential for agricultural and construction purposes.

A rather unusual, but not unique, feature was an underground canal, known as the Duke's Level, that served the dual purpose of drainage and transportation. It was driven into the hillside of Burbage at a height of 1170 feet and extended nearly a mile underground to the House Coal Seam. A barge, operated by a boy of about twelve, would travel into the hillside and return to fill the waiting carts in Level Lane.

From Axe Edge we follow paths and tracks to the head of the Dane, which will increasingly escort us until the moment when we turn homewards. The path takes us easily down to Orchard Farm and then by substantial tracks to Three Shires Head. This delightful spot hides a somewhat more sinister history. As the name suggests, the three counties of Cheshire, Derbyshire and Staffordshire converge at this point. In more rudimentary policing times, when the local constabulary had their jurisdiction limited to a particular county, the ne'er-do-wells would conduct their nefarious transactions at this point, confident that they could skip from one bank to another as it suited their purposes. In particular, the neighbouring village of Flash specialised in counterfeiting coins of the realm, hence the term Flash money, and used the Three Shires as a convenient outlet. Many years ago, the maternal antecedents of the writer farmed and feuded in the Wincle area and he was often sent fearful to sleep with, no doubt one-sided, stories of the dreaded Men from Flash ringing in his ears.

The momentum should be continued. Cross the bridge and a track takes you round the skirts of Turn Edge. At the apex, paths lead down fields to the road between Allgreave and Flash to Manor Farm. Pass through the farm and a track leads down to the Youth Hostel at Gradbach, where the river can be rejoined and followed into the woods of Back Forest. This means leaving the river for a little while whilst climbing to the ridge. This, in turn, runs easily down to Danebridge.

In the second half of the last stretch you have been in the Land of Oz. Lud's Church, which was a meeting place for the dissenting Lollards, is worth a diversion, but perhaps better explored on a separate occasion.The followers of Wycliffe might better be described as Heretics rather than Wizards but there is historical evidence that suggests that the narrow chasm was used in pagan days for rites more sinister than simply rebellion against the Establishment. The second connection is that you might see a wallaby. These escaped from a nearby private zoo, I suppose an early case of 'A Kangaroo is not just for Christmas', and successfully bred and survived in the wild. The press regularly report that they have been wiped out by winter conditions, only for them to reappear at a later date. Perhaps they go walkabout.

The full route, which would mean that you have, en passant, virtually completed the Gritstone Trail, should now follow the Dane, crossing a metal bridge to join a conduit which, in turn, leads to Barleigh Ford Bridge. At last, you turn north and head back to Macclesfield via the ruins of Dumkins and the farm at Hawkslee. This stretch can offer a sporting route, particularly after rain. The going can be graded as Mildly Amusing through Just Very Slippery to Extremely Annoying. No doubt the present day Aid-Men will not be above using the in-situ etriers to avoid the real challenge. However, as there is evidence of Motorway Construction on the southern end of the section, I am confident that in future publications it will appear as 'An Easy Day for a Lady'. To cut a corner, you can turn right at Danebridge and, passing through the village of Wincle, take a path or road to Wincle Grange. From here, stiles take you across fields to Dumkins or via Nettlebeds to Hawkslee itself. Now follow the top of Wincle Minn and drop down to the A54. Turn left and a lane shortly appears which will take you to the Radio Tower of Croker Hill. It is also possible to follow field paths that start immediately opposite the exit from the Minn and keep below the ridge of Sutton Common to join the Gritstone Trail at Lowerhouse.

As we are now in familiar territory, we can do as we wish. The complete walk would follow the Trail back to White Nancy, but the canal is at hand and it can be joined at various points to shorten the return journey.

Whatever you choose, you have covered a variety of ground and passed a variety of place names. Wincle Minn, for example, has two names: it is Wincle Minn on the east side, but Bosley Minn on the west. This is probably explained because the hill was named not by the locals but by foreigners who, on a clear day, could see it as an outstanding feature rising above the Cheshire Plain. They called it the Hill or, being Welsh, Mynydd. This would be corrupted to Mynd (as in Long Mynd) or Minn and the

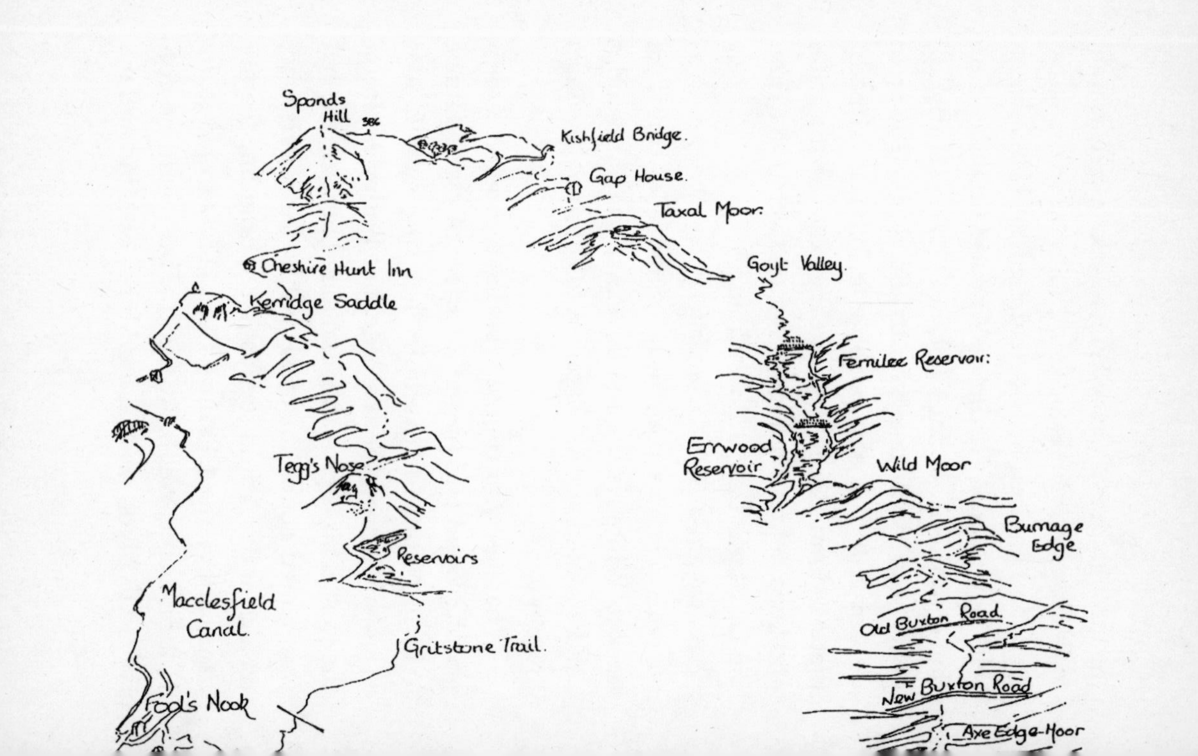
Sponds Hill
386
Kishfield Bridge.
Gap House.
Taxal Moor.
Cheshire Hunt Inn
Kerridge Saddle
Goyt Valley.
Fernilee Reservoir.
Errwood Reservoir
Wild Moor
Tegg's Nose
Reservoirs
Burnage Edge
Macclesfield Canal.
Gritstone Trail.
Old Buxton Road.
New Buxton Road
Fool's Nook
Axe Edge Moor

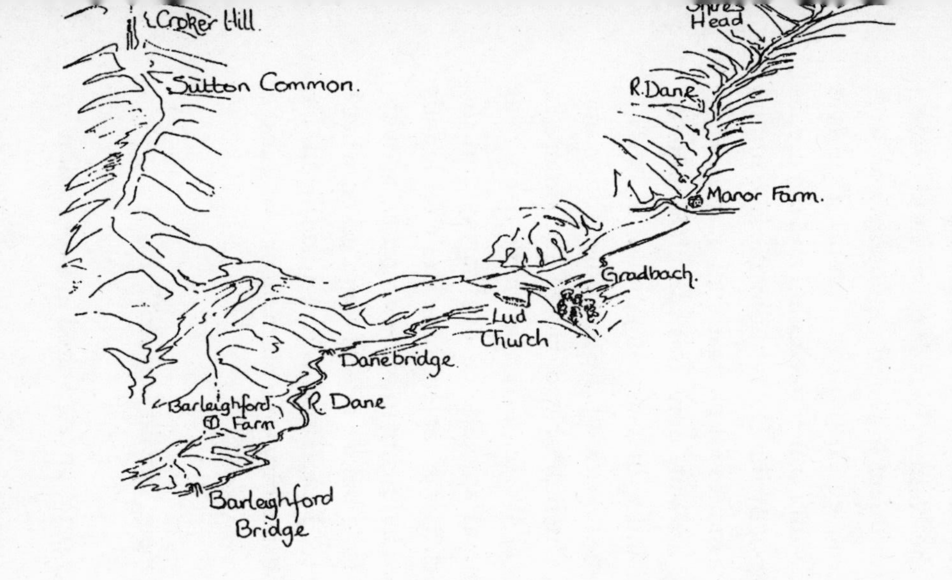

Route Five: A Lang Stride

land would be known as the Wincle or Bosley side of the Minn. This, in due time, would be collapsed into the present nomenclature. A similar state of affairs happened in the Western Islands of Scotland. Here a number of prominent hills and mountains end with the letters *-val*, eg Askival in Rhum. This is a Scandinavian suffix which means hill and the names were formed not by the Gaels but by the marauding Vikings, one assumes for navigational purposes.

The writer has only done this complete route on one occasion and with a certain amount of satisfaction slid down the side of the Kerridge Ridge into the hearth of The Bull's Head. Here I encountered a couple of Local Worthies. It must have been clear from my general appearance of disarray and the speed at which I was replenishing the vital liquids that I had been indulging in some strenuous activity, as it was not long before one of them asked what I had been up to. I explained where I had been. He considered the itinerary for a moment or two, sucked his pipe and remarked,

'Happen, that's a lang stride, lad.'

This latter-day φειδιππιδες waited in expectation for

elaboration, if not tribute. Another moment of cogitation.

'Ay.... But whurrer it get thee, sirree?'

As the poet said, 'In the end is my beginning.'

Part Two

The aim of Part One was to introduce the reader to the Macclesfield area and encourage the idea of Long Distance Walking. The order of the walks is supposed to allow a development of an understanding of the area and to increase the intensity of the challenge. Chapter Five, the circle of the district, is a lead-in to Part Two. This consists of three well known 'challenge' walks south of the Scottish Border. The first two are well documented and appear in what is the serious walker's *vade-macum* (given big enough pockets), Wilson and Gilbert's *The Big Walks.* They are within the reach of the determined and fit hill-walker, shorter than 'The Lang Stride', but with harder going and more up and down.

The Bob Graham Round is of a different order and, as I will suggest, the probable boundary for the walker as opposed to the athlete. The choice of these three is meant to be indicative rather than definitive.

The Bob Graham Round exists because Bob Graham decided to do it. Invent your own and plan the detail when you are stuck in a traffic jam.

Finally, Art includes Literature and much has been written about walking and climbing. Each of the following chapters will nod in this direction to a greater or lesser extent.

Six
The Derwent Watershed

As a walk, the nature of the Derwent Watershed is irrefutable; you start at point A, usually the Yorkshire Bridge (OS SK 197849), and continue on the highest ground you can find above the source of all streams until, provided you miss the bouncing bombs, you regain your starting point. The distance is forty miles.

The first section is more nursery rhyme than slope - up and down Win Hill to Twitchill Farm and then reascend to Lose Hill, down, not quite to the bottom, and up to Mam Tor. Perhaps the Grand Old Duke was a cartographer for this is the boundary of the White and Dark Peak. The limestone country to our left with its airy white rock and bright spring green grass is not for us. Far better are the bogs of Bleaklow and the marshes of Margery Hill for those who wish to sample True Grit. Nevertheless, at this stage, the way from Mam Tor and along Rushop Edge is easy going but, as the path swings towards the Kinder Plateau, there is a taste of things to come. From Brown Knoll slope down to Edale Cross and join the alternative start to the Pennine Way. The purist will continue steadfastly across the plateau to the summit of Kinder Scout and a bump called Crowden Head; the intelligent will follow an excellent path past the Downfall, which, because of the prevailing wind, as often goes Up, to the same point. The Snake Pass is the next objective attained via Mill Hill, where you will have the opportunity to meet up with any support party you have organised to provide refreshment at the appropriate temperature.

The Plastic Pennine Motorway is then followed to Bleaklow Head where the fun begins. From Bleaklow Head to Margery Hill is one of the roughest and most inhospitable bits of Britain south of Hadrian's Wall, and to keep to the watershed you have to take, as termed by the originators, 'some sharp corners' that lead annoyingly away from the general intended direction. The saving grace is that you are walking along a parish boundary and there are a series of marker stones to guide you on your way. Apart from these and the obligatory grice, there is little to catch the eye and it was, therefore, a moment of mutual surprise that turning a corner of a deep twisting grough on the north slopes of Margery Hill, I came face to face with a fox. This was not one of your Beatrice Potter foxes, all bushy tail and quizzical expression. This was a stringy alsatian sort of fox and the word 'rabid' sprang to mind. However, both parties were aware of the proper proportions of discretion and valour, with the vulpine Falstaff making the more graceful exit. Eventually, the land regains some definition and a ridge leads via Howden Edge and the head of Abbey Brook to Back Tor.

Now comes the moment of truth. The logical way home is to continue down the ridge of Derwent Edge to Ladybower House and thence to the starting point, but the Watershed needs to encompass streams running off Strines and Moscar Moors and a detour is required via Strines Inn, Moscar Lodge and Stanage High Neb before the walker descends over Bamford Edge to the Yorkshire Bridge Inn and a well deserved pint.

If you take the easier option you descend a pleasant rounded ridge that is ornamented with a series of appropriately named tors of weathered rock. After recrossing the Snake Road you take the A6013 towards Bamford until The Yorkshire Bridge Inn is reached. Those with the grit between the teeth will soldier on but may find passing interest in the activities taking place on the rock escarpments of Stanage and Bamford, where at most times of the year various groups gather to take part in a form of large scale macramé, accompanied by strange cries and counter cries. The former is a more likely venue than the latter as Bamford traditionally is an area of restricted access. In fact, the writer has been there on only three occasions. The first visit was in winter when I felt that the then severe restriction would be less fiercely policed. The snow and blue sky gave the day an Alpine flavour. There was even an extra edge of exploration as the only guide I had was a drawing of the cliff showing the climbing lines and grades. I thought the routes were, unusually for gritstone, overgraded but flattered myself that I must have been climbing well. On my second visit I discovered that the snow had drifted to such an extent that I had been stepping off the 'ground' twenty feet up the climb and usually on to or just above the crux. On the third and last occasion, there were further scenes from Shakespeare as I escaped the wrath of a man with an business-like gun.

It would be idle to suggest that the Peak District is

so named because of its position in a list of areas of outstanding natural beauty or that it refers to its shape, which, in the Dark Peak at least, is generally flat. Nor would it be correct to describe it as the Cinderella of the British Highlands, as the application of footwear tends to make matters worse than better. Nevertheless, it has its champions as is seen by this quaint prefatory remark employed by J Laycock in his *Some Shorter Climbs (1913),* a guide to some rock climbs in the area:

> *One can respect and adore the Queen of England and still love one's wife.*

The first of these champions was E A Baker whose book *Moors, Crags and Caves in the High Peak* (1903) set out to persuade his friends in the north that, if not as good as the Lake District, the Peak had much to recommend it as an area for climbing and walking. History shows that Baker was a false knight and something of a self-publicist whose motive for publication was to gain a place in the Pantheon of British Mountaineers. Indeed, a reading of the text would suggest that Baker, single-handed, opened up the district. This is not true, as the High Tor Gully episode reveals.

Writing for the Climbers' Club Journal, Baker singled out this fissure for particular praise, citing it as a 'noble gully'. The cliff of High Tor at Matlock is indeed imposing and its gully is probably the nearest thing the High Peak has to rival the 'classic' clefts of the Lake District crags. It was eventually climbed, not by Baker, who even after investigations on a top rope had been repulsed on previous occasions, but by, in national terms, an unknown climbing party. Baker immediately changed tack and dismissed the gully as a worthless rubbish chute.

The 'unknown party' was led by J W Puttrell who with his fellow silversmith W J Watson had opened up a variety of crags and produced climbs of a high standard. In his book Baker refers to them obliquely as his 'Sheffield friends' but never gives them the credit that was due. In fact the only names dropped are those that he hopes will impress. The following descriptions in a chapter on the climbs at Black Rocks reflect the tone:

> *Yet they are good climbs in their way, and their merits have been endorsed by the approval of several renowned climbers.*

and

> *I have seen a member of the Alpine Club totally unable to ascend a shorter but wider cleft (South Gully) that is a harder test of strength and skill.*

coupled with this description of Stonnis Crack, the 'non pareil' in his graded list of climbs, which had been led by Puttrell:

> *Though I have frequently ascended the Crack on a slack rope, I should say that to ascend it without a rope at all is a very dangerous and a perfectly useless feat.*

A closer inspection of his graded list of the Derbyshire 'Scrambles' is also revealing. He took the decision to omit the climbs on Wharncliffe, where Puttrell was king, on the grounds that they are much of a muchness and those on the Roaches because they 'have not yet acquired recognised names'. Perhaps, like the Alpinist, he found difficulty in getting off the ground. There is no mention at all of the climbs on Stanage, Froggatt, Bamford and Gardom's which had been completed by the Sheffield pair.

The record was finally set straight by the publication of a book to which much of this chapter is indebted, *High Peak - The Story of Walking and Climbing in the Peak District* by Eric Byne and Geoffrey Sutton (1966). This gives an even-handed view of where credit was deserved. It was the working (if they were lucky) classes that were setting the pace. Ultimately, the arrival on the scene of the Valkyrie Club and the emergence of Brown, Whillans et al dispelled any myths of superiority that Baker and his like had tried to perpetrate. The Unconquerables on Stanage Edge weren't and most of the last great problems went. The successful attempts on routes that were both bold and technically exacting had repercussions that changed the face of British climbing. The Old Guard could no longer maintain their aura by insisting that all novices started at the bottom of a graded list and respectfully worked their way up. The dominance of the University and other Established Clubs was not so much challenged as dismissively bypassed.

Parallel to this was the mass movement of the Right to Roam. The unemployed and underpaid on both sides of the Pennines saw walking in the Peak as an invigorating experience, and the founding of the Rucksack Club in Manchester and the Sheffield

Clarion Ramblers in 1902 stirred the slumbering landlord born of ancient rights or exploited labour when faced with a mass invasion of those who they had assumed were firmly bolted to the factory floor. More keepers were employed with the instruction to eject the trespasser. Confrontation was inevitable. The Clarion Ramblers, who had strong socialist leanings, saw the jealously guarded moors as bastions of privilege and power and were more than happy to challenge any keeper that tried to prevent their access. The 'Goliath' of the Ramblers was Bill Whitney, a pugilist, who took great delight in teasing the keepers who were too afraid of his reputed strength to retaliate. The owners' riposte was to publish photographs of ramblers, offering a reward for names, addresses and, most ominously, occupations of the persons so identified. The fact that the pose of the persons involved indicated that they were on friendly terms with the photographer would suggest that the landlords had a somewhat perfidious 'David'.

Whatever political implications might have existed, the serious walkers were unconcerned and continued to roam far and wide. The early leading light was Cecil Dawson, known to all as the 'Colonel'. He and his friends, described collectively as the '94th',

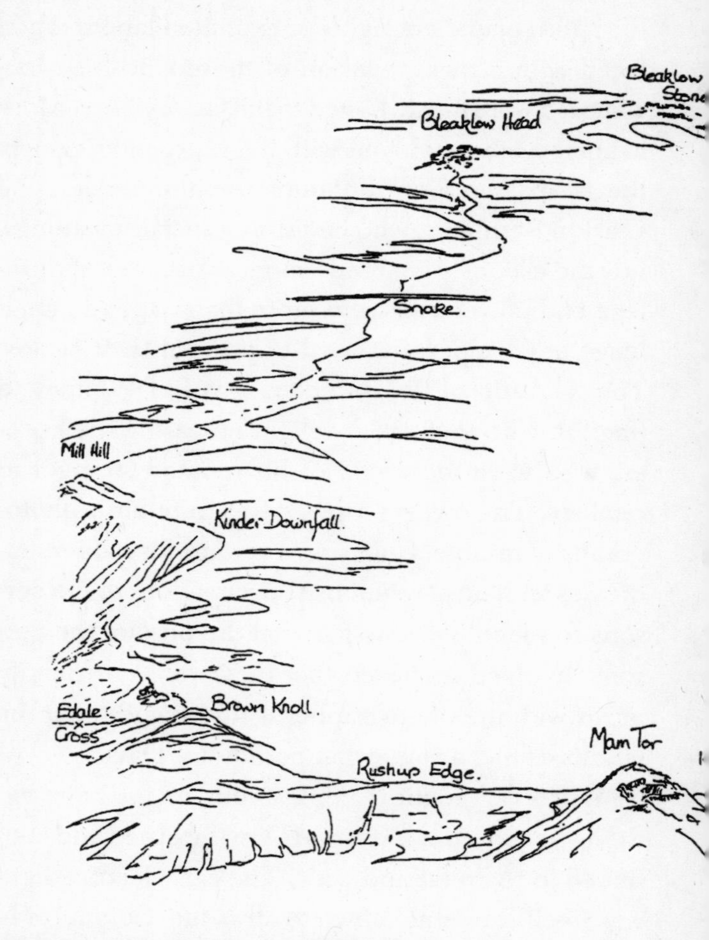

Route Six: The Derwent Watershed

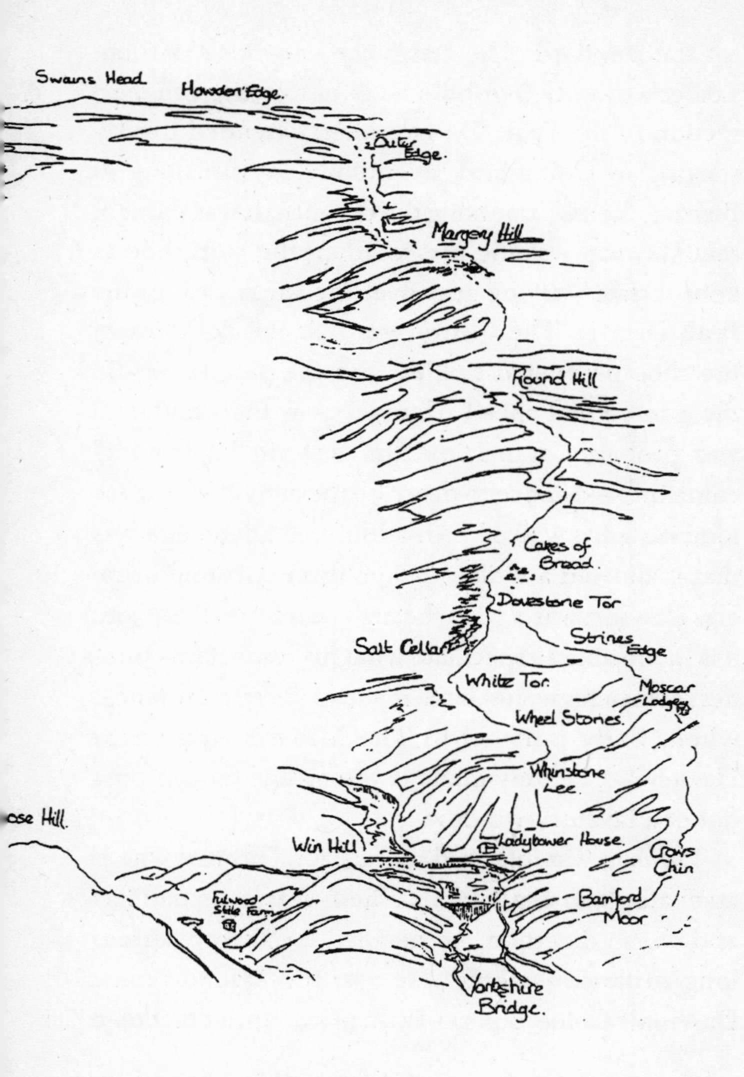
Swains Head
Howden Edge.
Outer Edge.
Margery Hill
Round Hill
Cakes of Bread.
Dovestone Tor
Salt Cellar
Strines Edge
White Tor.
Moscar Lodge
Wheel Stones.
Whinstone Lee.
ose Hill.
Win Hill
Ladybower House.
Crows Chin
Fulwood Stile Farm
Bamford Moor
Yorkshire Bridge.

set the standard. The test piece was the Marsden-Edale, a twenty-five mile walk across the roughest section of the Peak. Dawson then extended this by starting at Colne and, eventually, by finishing at Buxton, thereby doubling the distance. It was thought that Dawson was the first to adopt the gym shoe as appropriate walking gear over the soggy peat of the Peak District. The theory was that the lightness of the shoe prevented sinking into the morass, as did the consequent speed of travel over the ground. It was, probably, at this time that the term 'bogtrotting' came into existence to describe the activities of these long distance walkers. An additional advantage was that it allowed a swifter escape from pursuing keepers. Dawson was a Manchester cotton merchant and it is interesting to speculate what his respectable business associates would have made of the circumstances when, hotly pursued to The Miller's Arms near Hazlehead, he only managed to escape by climbing out of a lavatory window.

Dawson was followed by Eustace Thomas, who is an example to us all. In his fiftieth year, with bad feet and worse digestion, he decided to take up serious long distance walking. He was the first to repeat Dawson's Colne-Buxton Walk in just under eighteen hours and, with several friends, worked out and completed the Watershed Walk of this chapter, for many years the toughest walk in the area. After surpassing Wakefield's round in the Lake District (of which more later) he took to the Alps, and was the first Englishman to climb all eighty-three summits that exceeded 4000 metres. Age, however, takes its toll and by the time he was ninety, he was reduced to taking up flying and making the odd polar traverse.

As a trained engineer, he adopted a scientific approach to the art of long distance walking. In the Rucksack Club Journal of 1921, he wrote an article entitled 'Mountain Endurance'. In this, he examined the source of energy and the nature of fatigue. He realised that the food consumed in the weeks before a Race and food on the Day had different purposes and that it was essential in training to develop the chest expansion to aid breathing (he managed a 50% improvement). Most importantly he recognised the importance of 'buffer salts' which helped break down 'clogging fatigue products'. Although all this was known to scientists, it was little appreciated by athletes and Thomas' investigations show that the ageing process does not necessarily impair endurance and strength. Perhaps he was at his most 'modern' in his understanding of Sports Psychology. This account of the week before the Race, mercifully free of today's jargon, illustrates the point:

> *This was spent in Borrowdale, with exercises, and plenty of sleep and rest. A feeling of funk was fought back. Mental and physical relaxing, awake and asleep, were sought after, and massage taken each day. A great tuning-up took place, as much nervous as physical, to a level much above the normal.*

But, as an engineer, he specifically examined the Mechanics of Walking:

> *Engineers must not judge walking and climbing by foot-pounds only. Mere effort alone is fatiguing. So deep knee-bending is very tiring. Hence an unusually short step was developed for steep ascents to diminish knee-bending. Those muscles should be developed which sway the hips and by which one can walk upstairs without bending the knees. On the level a long racing step seems desirable, and may be alternated with trotting. Down hill, rapid shortish steps reduce jarring and conserve condition for the end of the course.*

All this preparation enabled him to break the record of Lakeland summits that could be attained on foot within twenty-four hours, starting and finishing at Keswick. He ascended over 25,000 feet and extended the course. Not content with that, he continued for a further four and a half hours to achieve one of his private ambitions, a total ascent of 30,000 feet. The complete distance was seventy-nine miles. Or, to put it a different way, he had run three marathons and climbed Mount Everest without stopping for a significant rest. The only comment he offered on the walk itself was less than detailed:

> *The night was clear and cold, but the tops from Bowfell to Saddleback were traversed in cloud. Some rain fell.*

If Dawson set the tone, then Thomas raised the pace. Of the many that followed, two stand out. Fred Heardman, licensee of The Nag's Head at Edale, made the first double Marsden-Edale, a feat that was not often repeated in the following thirty years. He then, accompanied by Harold Gerrard and John Burton, set out to extend the classic linear route, which Dawson had started at Colne, as far as Rowsley.

They began this journey of seventy-three miles at four o'clock on a Saturday afternoon and the aim was to catch the last train home which left Rowsley at 9.30 on Sunday night. They did it with a quarter of an hour to spare. However, Heardman left not only the legacy of his walks, but also the Edale Valley in its present unviolated state. As a member of the Rural District Council he fought a long and eventually successful battle against powerful business interests that wished to introduce industrialisation into the area. In those days it must have been a lone and thankless task and the inner strength needed so often in his tramps across Kinder and Bleaklow must have served him well in his fight against powerful financial and vested interests.

The second was Alf Bridge, a good rock climber and an outstanding walker who visited Macclesfield at least twice, once starting at Penistone and on another occasion at Greenfield. He covered long distances and he walked quickly - his average time for the Marsden-Edale was four hours - but his most impressive journey was a climbing/bivouacking/walking excursion which started at Greenfield after work on Saturday lunchtime to catch the nine o'clock train on Sunday evening at Chinley. In between these times, he visited the crags of Laddow, Stanage, Cratcliffe Tor and Castle Naze and did three of the harder rock climbs on each. It is worth getting out the OS one-inch Tourist Map of the Peak District to see for yourself what this involved. A crow would start at the top left hand corner and flap its way to Birchover, near Matlock, at the bottom right and return to Chinley, overflying the White Peak, a distance of 100 corvine miles. Of course the crow would not be inconvenienced by the odd hill or reservoir that might get in the way but would rightly feel that it had something to, whatever verb crows use when particularly pleased with themselves, about on its return.

Bridge's 'tour de force' should remind us that these feats of endurance and athleticism were done in more demanding times than ours. All those who worked did so until Saturday lunchtime and failure to catch the last train home on Sunday could have serious or at least wearisome repercussions. Today's use of the car or cars to drop you off and pick you up at convenient points makes many of these outings that much easier, as does the opportunity to take the odd day off to recuperate. Whether the going is better or worse is a matter for debate, but it was and is never easy.

Peat is intractable stuff. Unless it is frozen, or at the end of a long dry, hot spell, it has a way of its own; the avoidance of the worst bogs and the slipping and sliding around the groughs on the ground will put measurable distance on to that shown on the map.

An indication of these conditions can be gleaned from a light-hearted account that appeared in the 1937 Rucksack Journal entitled 'Of Bogs, Swamps and Quagmires' and written by S F Forrester. In a scathing attack, he put the literary horrors of Grimpen Mire and Cranmere Pool down to an over-indulgence of poetic licence on the parts of Doyle and Blackmore and went so far as to state that there was no such a thing as a dangerous bog in Great Britain, let alone the Peak District. This, naturally, led to a counter-claim:

> *A friend of mine held diametrically opposite views and a heated discussion took place resulting in the betting of a quart of bitter followed by a rather sporting event of which the conditions were: (1) he should select the juiciest spot he could find; (2) this should not be the red iron stuff owing to the stink and general mess that would result therefrom; (3) I should take a running jump into his choice at a marked*

spot. It was some months before the event came off, owing to the difficulty of his final selection; and even then when he had me on the ground he was not certain which of the two remaining on his short list he should take. Lot one had firm ground at one side; lot two had not, but looked a bit more succulent. This last fact appealed to him and he voted for lot two. I had no objection but pointed out the impossibility of complying with condition (3) above. He saw the force of this observation and said he would be content with lot one. He threw a match-stalk onto the exact spot where he wished me to alight; it was about six feet from the edge and was about one foot above the green skin. He expressed doubts as to whether I should go through the skin but thought it likely; so he exhorted me to jump high and shook hands with me for what he said might be the last time. Everything being now in order I took a five-yard run, made a charming take-off, hit the match beautifully, went successfully through the skin and sank slowly to equilibrium. This resulted in immersion to just above my knees - rather deeper than I had expected, but legs, body and head less than he hoped. I was able to get out without help, so there must have been some sort of bottom, although I cannot recollect it. The bet was duly liquidated (to my satisfaction) at a place provided for the purpose.

The following years leading up to the Second World War saw an explosion of outdoor activity fuelled by the Depression and it has been estimated that as many as 15,000 people flooded into the Peak District on an average Sunday from Manchester alone, and probably as many again from the other side of the Pennines. As can be imagined, the clashes between keepers and ramblers escalated, ending with a number of the latter being imprisoned. What particularly annoyed the walkers and climbers was that they were prevented from entering public land controlled by the Water Board on the ground that there was a danger of pollution, a danger that immediately disappeared when the land was used for shooting purposes by the Landed Gentry. The struggle for Access continued but it was not until 1951 that the Peak District became Britain's first National Park.

It was at around this time that a final wave of exploration took place. In order to celebrate the Silver Jubilee of the Rucksack Club, a club party followed Fred Heardman's suggestion of linking the two highest inns in England, The Tan Hill and The Cat and

Fiddle, and the 120 mile epic was completed in a little over fifty-four hours. At the same time, the National Parks and Access to the Countryside Act allowed an outline approval for the Pennine Way. The formation of the Mountain Club based in Stafford pushed back the boundaries still further. In 1953 'Larry' Lambe and John Sumner completed the High Peak Horseshoe route, ie following the horseshoe of Dark Peak gritstone that surrounds the limestone centre of the White Peak. This started at Hen Cloud near Leek, joined and completed the northern arc of the Derwent Watershed and finished, via the gritstone edges, at Matlock railway station. Three years later the club completed the Three Rivers Walk, up the Dane, down the Manifold and back up the Dove. This, with a similar exploration of the Wye and Derwent, neatly filled in the space occupied by the Dales within the Horseshoe and brought fifty odd years of long distance walking to a suitable moment of fruition. Others may have gone further and faster since then, but the real struggles had been fought and won.

Seven

The Welsh Threethousanders

The compact nature of Britain is reflected in its mountainous areas. Not least in Snowdonia, where the highest hills of Wales form a convenient group. It is an obvious target to climb all the fourteen mountains over 3000 feet and eventually to ascend them all in one go. They are divided into three sub-groups. The peaks of Snowdon, Yr Wyddfa, Crib-y-Ddysgl and Crib Goch are clustered tightly together but connected by narrow, at times knife-edged, ridges. The Big and Little Glyder are flanked by Elidir Fawr and Y Garn to the north-west and Tryfan to the north-east. The Carneddau form the final arm that sprawls towards the bay at Conway and contains the six remaining summits. The three groups are separated by the passes of Llanberis and Nant Ffrancon. The distance is twenty-four miles and the total ascent is in the region of 8,500 feet, assuming you start at the top of Snowdon and finish at the summit of Foel Fras.

It is probable that the traverse had been done on many occasions but it was brought to the public notice by a successful bid on the 'record' by Tom Firbank, a Canadian who in 1933 had bought a sheep farm on the slopes of Glyder Fach. He recorded his experiences in an autobiographical account entitled *I Bought A Mountain.* Not inhibited by the English disease of false modesty, he recounts the ups and downs of Welsh sheep farming with refreshing honesty. It has recently been republished and is to be recommended as an interesting and informed insight into a mountainous area where you live and work rather than visit to play.

In a chapter heralded as 'The Record Walk' he describes the successful attempt by himself and his companions on the record, which stood at that time at twelve and a half hours. Unencumbered by tradition, Firbank laid down the ground rules stated above. He also stipulated that no mechanical aid was to be used. The party worked out split times and investigated alternative ways of ascent and descent and reached the point that, if they could sustain their best efforts over the whole course, they would break the record with an hour to spare. This complacency was wiped out when they discovered that they had overlooked Yr Elen, that lies out on a limb from the main Carneddau range. The additional time necessary to accomplish this swallowed their cushion. But worse was to follow: someone else had reduced the time to ten and a half hours. Activity was stepped up; corners were cut both literally and into the margins of safety. But it was still too close to call and, try as they might, they could make no real inroads into the wearisome traverse across the boulder-strewn slopes from the top of Pen-y-pass to the slopes of Elidir Fawr. It was at this point that Firbank's wife, Esmé, had a moment of lateral feminine thinking. She suggested that, rather than maintain height by traversing the awful terrain of Esgair Felen, they should head straight down the road to Nant Peris and begin the ascent of Elidir from there. As this meant the loss of about 1000 feet, with the commensurate reascent, the men scoffed. Esmé tried it. The result: a net gain of thirty minutes saved.

Eventually, the appointed day arrived. A train was hired to take them to the top of Snowdon. The BBC and the national press trumpeted. The real mountaineers sniffed and retired to their tents at Helyg. The description of the attempt follows at the same breakneck speed as the journey - they scaled the crests of Cribs y Ddysgl and Goch - plunged down the North Ridge into the Pass - swept past the spectators of the 'Great Race' in Nant Peris - almost missed in the mist the cairn of Elidir - thundered on to the Glyders - repeated the mantra on Tryfan - leapt with a single bound into the Ogwen Valley - cramp in the Carnedds - Llewellyn... Foel Grach... Fras - and the outcome was that they completed the ascents in just under eight and a half hours. Interviews were given and the matter was, as far as Firbank was concerned, forgotten. The mountaineers reappeared and continued their siege on the mist-girt cliffs of Bochlwyd Buttress and the Gribin Facet.

It has, as you would expect, been done faster. Joss Naylor covered the course in under five hours but Firbank's time is still a decent one to aim for. If you want to make it a circular trip, you can park at the Pen-y-Gwyrd and make your way to the top of Snowdon from there. After completing the fourteen peaks, you could return under the crags of Craig yr Ysfa and take the climbers' track back to the foot of Tryfan. Here the Miners' Track can be picked up and the upper slopes of Glyder Fach can be crossed to reach your vehicle.

Firbank's upbeat approach is at odds with the

Route Seven : The Welsh Threethousanders

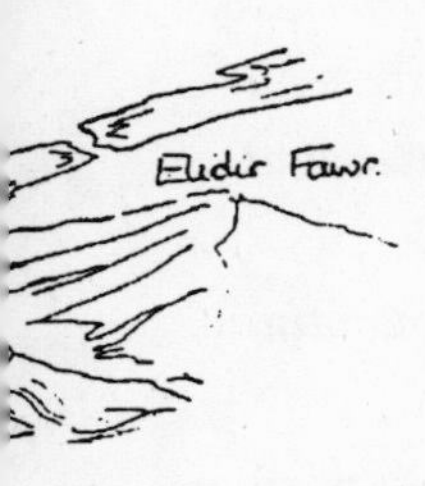
Elidir Fawr.

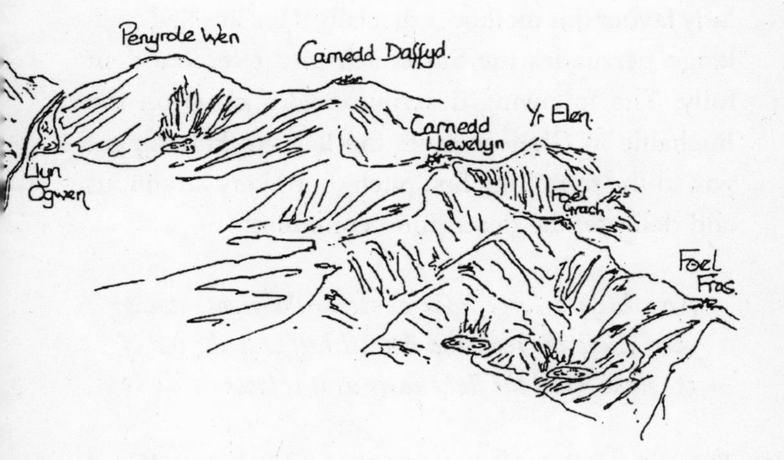
Penyrole Wen
Carnedd Daffyd.
Carnedd
Llewelyn
Yr Elen.
Llyn
Ogwen
Foel
Grach
Foel
Fras.

literary style that is typical of British mountaineering. As the scale of our native hills does not allow the epic mode, viz:

> *Having crossed the heavily crevassed glacier, we peered into the depths of the bergschrund and wondered how we might effect a purchase on the 500 foot ice-wall that loomed above us. Base Camp and its attendant comforts seemed a very, very long way away.*
>
> (from *Llà-Dos: The Last Lost Mountain*)

there is a tendency to the laconic. The Scots particularly favour this method, especially if the implied challenge persuades the Sassenach into overconfident folly. The following description of a route on the Buchaille in Glencoe gives the flavour. Having got you to the top of the first pitch (both very strenuous and delicate) the description continues:

> *Now lasso a large flake above to the right, swing over, climb the rope and mantelshelf onto the top of the flake. Quit the flake early as it is loose.*

This approach is all very well but it tends to pall and is open to obvious parody:

I had reached the crux of the climb when I became aware of a not inconsiderable amount of loose rock making its way down the cliff face. A portion of this struck me on the right shoulder, resulting in a minor dislocation of the joint. This was not as serious as I first feared as the only reasonable hold was for the left hand and the fortuitous extension of the right limb enabled me to take advantage of a pressure hold which otherwise I would have been unable to reach. I soon settled into a belay constructed around off-set notches and brought up my second. Fortunately Ogilvie-Smythe-Ffoulkes recalled some rudimentary medical training that he had acquired whilst serving in the Bengal Lancers and he soon had everything back in working order. I felt, in any event, there was little cause for concern as the rock had receded to the vertical and the hairline crack that started a few metres above my head seemed to continue unbroken to the top of the cliff.

(from *Some Scrambles Outwith the Scottish Mainland)*

What, then, is the 'Great Tradition' of British Mountaineering Literature? In common with most, the canon has two sources, the oral and the written.

Unlike most, one does not develop from the other and they are quite separate in their ambitions. The latter finds its roots in the Journals kept by the Victorians on holiday in the Alps. In her essays on photography, Susan Sontag suggests that members of societies, driven by the work ethic, are unhappy to go on holiday and do nothing. They need an acceptable substitute for 'work' and find that taking pictures, with its attendant chores, fills the bill, or, in this case, writing a report on their activities in a pseudo-scientific manner.

The simplest form of the written is the guide book. By and large this is a harmless volume and, with one or two exceptions (the Cloggy guide of 1963 was reviewed as 'more gripping than the latest James Bond'), of no real literary interest. This approach was expanded into a commentary on the events and feelings of the guide book writer. At their best, these can be inspirational to the young and stoke up the afterglow of the aged. Without doubt, W H Murray's *Mountaineering in Scotland* and its companion piece, *Undiscovered Scotland*, have done more than most to excite the imagination, as has, in its more understated way, L J Oppenheimer's *Heart of Lakeland*. Sometimes such works can act as benchmarks by which the sport can judge itself. Haskett-Smith's ascent of the totem pole of the F&RCC is a good example. However, there is tendency to degeneration - Chapter One: The Trek to Base Camp, Chapter Two: Camp Two, Chapter Three: Did We See a Yeti? etc. It is probably true to say that, despite the best efforts of *The Reader's Digest*, this branch has withered and died.

This does not mean that the moving finger has ceased to write but that its source is now the oral tradition, a tradition given to a sceptical examination of the received code of practice invented by the senior climbing clubs, cf The Apocrypha of Whillans. At first this was anecdotal, stories repeated in bivouacs and pubs to pass the time or impress the opposite sex with their gallows humour. Two that relate to the activities of The Creagh Dhu, a rather loose-knit Scottish Climbing Club, will serve to illustrate a point. On the first occasion, seeing a fellow member in evident difficulty and about to part company from the rock and, no doubt, do himself, at best, serious injury, his companion dived into his tent, reappearing with a bugle on which he proceeded to play The Last Post. On the second, the climber, also soloing, found himself in a similar situation and politely suggested that 'he could do with a rope'. This duly arrived, uncoiled, having been dropped on his head from the top of the cliff. Whether these are true or not is irrelevant; they are seminal to the state of modern mountaineering writing. The first accepts the fact that if you place yourself of your own volition in dangerous situations any unfortunate consequences cannot be described as heroic; the second that sang-froid, with its associated code of behaviour, was only thought to be meritorious because the products of the English Public School system had to be given some explanation as to why their parents chose to pay substantial sums of money for them to suffer living conditions they wouldn't have inflicted on their servants, let alone the livestock.

An interesting early volley is found in the much anthologised short story by C E Montague, *A Botanist in Hanging Garden Gully*. It starts with a climber convalescing from some unspecified sickness at an inn in North Wales who, despite the medical advice to 'avoid all violent exercise' persuades himself that he is fit enough to attempt the rock climb named in the title. To ignore medical advice is, as we all know, easy. It is perfectly reasonable to assume that it is probably erring on the safe side to avoid unpleasant legal repercussions. But there was a more serious prohibition that could not be so lightly dismissed. It was considered to be the height of irresponsibility to climb without a companion and if anything unfortunate were to happen, the wrath of the climbing world would fall on your head and most other pieces of your anatomy. As the narrator observes:

> *If, as the Greeks so delicately put it, anything incurable happens while you are climbing alone, your clay is exposed, defenceless and dumb, to nasty 'obiter dicta' during the inquest.*

It is no difficult matter to fail to take your medicine, but it is an entirely different affair to be, even posthumously, drummed out of the Climbing Club.

However, the dilemma was resolved by the arrival at the inn of a one-legged botanist or, rather, a botanist with only one sound leg, whose ultimate aim in life was to find a specimen of flower that grew solely in the area. As his presence at the bottom end of the rope would dispense with objection number two, the narrator persuades his fellow resident to accompany him on the chosen climb by assuring the enthusiast that this 'eccentric' plant would most certainly be found there. His plan backfired. The botanist, seeing a single sprig of his beloved plant clinging precariously to a crack in an otherwise featureless rockface, set off at the double, or should it be said single, to retrieve it. The leader, secure at the top of the climb, had previously threaded the rope behind two chockstones and, in order to allow his second to climb outside these, had him tied to both ends of a doubled rope. The result of these precautions was that if the botanist, now no longer protected by a rope from above, should fall, he would swing with disastrous effect back on to the chimney wall. Although this calamity is averted, another occurs. The circle of rope runs out and all matters come to a stop, jammed fast. As this is now on easy ground, they are able to unrope and make their way to the foot of the cliff by a simple walking route. However, the rope is still festooning the climb for all to see and there is only one worse sin than climbing solo and that is to leave your gear in such a manner that it signifies an undignified retreat. So the narrator consoles himself that he will be perfectly justified in returning alone the next day to salvage the rope.

At first sight, the story seems to support the narrator's comparative assessment of his climbing party - 'the man who had gone mad on the greenstuff and the man who knew what was what' - and it can superficially appear as a tale of the innocent abroad, saved only by the sophistication of a man of the world. But a more careful analysis shows a different authorial intention. The satire on climbing and climbers is clear. They can be essentially self-centred individuals who seize the moral high ground when it suits them and abandon it likewise. The threading of the rope round the chockstones, ostensibly to control the inexperienced second, is, of course, to protect the leader. The choice of climb was to fulfil the climber's rather than the botanist's ambition, as is shown by the twist to the tale. The narrator sits on the final belay 'in the heaven that big game hunters know when they lie up against the slain tiger and smoke', oblivious to a positive field of the desired flower that lies around him. That the route can be 'soloed' the next day with the security of a pulley placed above all difficulty puts him in the pantheon of 'Whymper, Tyndall and others' who in an earlier part of the story were considered exempt from the general diktat. Finally, the mocking of the botanist and his ilk, with its nudge and a wink to the complicit reader, serves only to underline the sanctimonious nature of the judge. In fact, the real story, writ small, is that an egocentric and incompetent climber only avoids a serious mishap because of the superior climbing skills of an incapacitated novice.

This vein of satire runs through much of the best British mountain writing. W E Bowman, with his *Ascent of Rum Doodle* adopts the mock-epic mode; G C E Dutton's *The Ridiculous Mountains* exploits the possibilities of a mountainous sit com and Alastair Borthwick's *Always a Little Further* keeps the Scottish sardonic streak alive. Sometimes the humour can act as a cover for more serious matters. The life and writings of Menlove Edwards, the two of which are bound inextricably, are a case in point. Edwards, a psychiatrist, saw that the activities of the climber reflected in sharp relief the behaviour of mankind in general. 'End of A Climb', an essay written for the Climbers' Club Journal 1937, supports this assertion. The allegorical nature of the piece is clear, as this description of the 'Idwal Slab' shows:

> *Dreams of a little people. I remember a boy we saw climbing two or three times, on the Idwal Slabs. He would stand and gaze at the foot of the rocks, scanning them to right and left for some path in their expanse that the foot of man had not yet utilised.*

Then he went to the foot of the Ordinary Route. As he ascended, however, it was clear enough that he was no ordinary climber, for every now and then he stood, and looked around him with that air of expectancy that is the true explorer's heritage. We realised that at any moment, maybe without the least warning, he might break out on to fresh ground. Rather to our surprise he did actually continue up the Ordinary Route. Perhaps there was something in store for us now, for there he was, gazing with a wide purview above, below and to either side. The preliminaries were over. Clearly he knew these cliffs well, but was now eager above all things for fresh endeavour, new pasture. Sure enough, he made no pause for rest, but turned round and with every appearance of one whose mind is set to conquer or to die, he made his way laboriously down Ordinary Route. We laughed at him at the time and called him the Idwal Slab.

In a similar manner, 'A Great Effort' (CCJ 1941) relentlessly examines man's infinite capacity for excuses and self-justification. At the point where the extract takes up the account, the writer is fifteen feet off the ground and in a state of uncertainty:

But any man must be to some degree hard-pressed before he gives up on a point where his heart is set; so I began to struggle. Oh, good heavens, good heavens, I thought, what on earth am I to do; this is not very good, you are being a coward, an arrant coward and this cannot, must not, continue. I have time and again pointed out to you that you are being very silly but you do nothing, you do nothing except stand there with that fixed and ridiculous stare a few feet from the foot of this wretched precipice. But I still accomplished nothing. Then I began to struggle again. I thought, what is wrong, there is something missing, there is no spirit, I am heavy and unable to move; perhaps if I launch out and become sufficiently frightened; in fact I am sure that once over the border there would be no holding me. So I made several attempts to launch out, but nothing happened. Then I thought perhaps if I eat my sandwiches that will improve me, but no no for shame, it is not yet half past eleven, how can I eat them now, yet there can be no harm in it, give yourself a change, I said, eat them all and that will be a load off your mind, then you will not have the temptation to eat again until you get home. So, standing still on my footholds and feeling firmer than I had done for some time, I got the tin of sar-

dines out of my pocket, twisted the lid off in the usual way but carefully because of the position and ate the fish one by one with my mouth.

Eventually he gives up the unequal struggle and makes a humiliating retreat.

But the resilience of man is great, and his ingenuity. So I was not done yet and on the way back setting to work I soon picked up my pride in this way, by thinking, today the victory has been to the devil, but tomorrow is not to him yet, also by thinking: it has been said that the secret of life is in detachment from it, good.

All this must be read in the context that Edwards was a, if not the, leading climber of his time. His various exploits are catalogued in two volumes, *Samson* by Noyce and Sutton, and *Menlove*, a more forthright account by Jim Perrin.

In his less introspective moments, his touch is light and the extract from 'Young Climbers' (CCJ 1934) that describes the loose and dangerous cliffs of the Devil's Kitchen denies my earlier premise that guide books are inevitably boring:

But to get to the routes, the Devil's Kitchen group, Clogwyn-y-Geifr is an interesting spot, and may be dispensed with quickly, as the guide to it hopes to be coming out soon. It has every natural advantage, being steep, composed of pretty rocky sort of rock and being covered with vegetation: also parts of it have been long overdue for public exploitation. It is the sort of place where one can feel the full glory of stepping in perfect safety on somebody else's considered opinion. It is not of course the cliff for those who attack the problem tooth and nail nor yet for those who rise by seizing every opportunity, but I think it may now be considered safe for democracy. It is years since anybody was killed there.

After his sudden death in 1958, it was left to another member of the medical profession to pick up the cudgels. Tom Patey, who was killed in a climbing accident in 1970, left behind him a series of essays which have been collected together under the title of *One Man's Mountains*, a title that evokes the ghost of Edwards with its implications of both the Possessor and Possessed. In 'Apes or Ballerinas?' Patey debunks the idea of Climber as Graceful Athlete/Male Model and in 'The Greatest Show on Earth', with its TV armchair guide to mountaineering, and 'The Shape of Things to Come', he gives a humorous but real warning of the onset of commercialism. His predecessors may have exposed the posturing behind the codes and practices of the Amateur Sporting Gentleman, but once you remove the walls of hallowed tradition, it will not be long before the breach is filled by those who 'fumble in the greasy till'.

Not that the old brigade escaped entirely. He sorts out solitary climbing once and for all:

> *Venerable Proposition 1: Thou shalt not climb alone;*
> *Venerable Proposition 2: A Leader must* never *fall;*
> *Obvious Conclusion: As the Leader will never fall, there is no danger in climbing solo.*

and in 'The Art of Climbing Down Gracefully', a symposium of commonly used ploys …

> *The 'Ice-Man' Ploy:*
> *This is the exiled Scotsman's counter-ploy when lured on to English outcrops. 'I'm a Snow and Ice Man myself!' is a fairly safe assertion at Harrison's where it is highly unlikely that you will be given the opportunity to demonstrate your skills.*

Oddly enough the first time I heard this line it was spoken by an Englishman. The scene was an Alpine hut, at that time (1952) almost entirely populated by Oxbridge types - pleasant fellows, although all unmistakably tarred with the same brush, and handicapped by their common background. Amid this select group one particular rank outsider stuck out like a sore thumb. I was captivated by his facility for saying the wrong thing at the wrong time. ('I say! You two lads have got definite promise. If one of you gets himself killed would the other please look me up? I'm looking for a partner for the Brenva.')

This man had swallowed Smythe and Murray piecemeal and could regurgitate selected phrases from either author with gay abandon. His impact on the Establishment was shattering: 'All this talk of VIs and A3s bores me to tears,' he would announce in a loud voice, addressing no one in particular. 'Show me the Englishman - Yes; show me the Englishman, I say - who can stand upright in his steps, square set to the slope, and hit home hard and true, striking from the shoulder! There must be very few of us Ice-Men left around. Ice-Manship may be a forgotten craft but it's still the Cornerstone of Mountaineering. Never forget that! Any fool can monkey around on rock overhangs but it takes craft and cunning to beat the Brenva!'

He got away with it too. The 'Great Mixed Routes' are so seldom in condition that a dedicated Ice-man can remain in semi-permanent cold storage without much fear of exposure.

Of course, other sporting pastimes have their literature, but it is usually either instructional - *1001 Ways to Improve your Golf Swing* - or triumphalist - *United: the March through Europe, Volume 36*. Mountaineering, with the possible exception of cricket through (inter alia) the pens of Cardus and Arlott, offers the widest variety and range. It is interesting that these, apparently disparate, activities should share this common bond. However, there are moments of contact. First, unlike most athletic pursuits, they are not played at pace. There is time for reflection; strategies can be developed, codes of conduct can be expected; analysis can be made. Second, the lack of success does not necessarily mean failure. To draw a game of cricket under certain circumstances can be more worthy than winning in others. To find such a parallel with climbing needs no more than a perusal of Patey's account of 'A Short Walk with

Whillans'. Third, although others are involved in fielding, one way or the other, the efforts of others, both are activities that depend on the skill, judgement and determination of the individual. There is no second chance, no opportunity to make amends. When you fail you are 'out'. You can no more ask for 'three bat handles' on the north face of the Eiger than you can in Sabina Park, Jamaica.

Eight

The Bob Graham Round

Despite its name this is not, by nature, a fixed, predetermined round but, rather, a round fixed in a moment of time and space. Its genesis has two strands: peakbagging, eg climbing all the Lakes' 3000ers in one go, which would require a start from point A and taking the shortest route possible to reach point B; the 'round', ie traversing a cirque of hills, starting and finishing at the same spot. There is no record of who completed the former but the Rev J M Elliott is credited with the invention of the latter concept when, in 1864, he set off from Wasdale and completed a circuit that took in Scafell, Great Gable, Pillar and Red Pike before returning to base in a time of eight and a half hours. It took Thomas Watson to combine the two by starting and finishing in Keswick and climbing as many summits as possible within twenty-four hours. This feat set the ground rules for 'record' attempts on the Lakeland Peaks. This, as has been mentioned earlier, was variously held by Dr Wakefield and in 1920 by Eustace Thomas, who covered Wakefield's Round but in a shorter time.

Such was the state of play when in 1932 Bob Graham, a guest house proprietor in Keswick, made his attempt. However, he took a different approach from his predecessor. Rather than attempting to beat Thomas' time, he decided that he would increase the length of the course to forty-two summits, one for each year of his life. The result was a journey of seventy-two miles and 27,000 feet of ascent and he returned to Keswick with twenty minutes to spare. At the time of its completion it appeared to be no more than a milestone which would be overtaken in due course, more likely sooner than later. However, it stood for twenty-eight years and as time passed became regarded more and more as a definitive challenge. That is, something to do in its own right rather than a time to be beaten. Of course, people have now gone faster and additional summits have been added but the levels that have been attained are more akin to serious athletics than athletic fell-walking and the round that Graham did is a tough but reasonable target for the fit and trained hill-walker who is prepared to run the flat and downhill.

The whole affair was further set in stone with the birth of the Bob Graham Twenty-Four Hour Club. In 1972 the club had just nine members. Twenty years later there were 750. This number, like the Compleat Munroists, will no doubt, given improved leisure and a lengthening active life-style, continue to grow at an ever-increasing rate.

So what is the Bob Graham Round? As stated, it must start and finish in Keswick and be completed within twenty-four hours. The summits can be completed in any order, but in practical terms this only gives you the choice of doing them clockwise or anti-clockwise. Clockwise, the round falls into five groups. First, the triangle of Skiddaw, Great Calva and Blencathra, followed by a drop to Threlkeld. Second, a relatively easy traverse of the Dodds, Helvellyn and Fairfield plus satellites before descending to Dunmail Raise. Third, once High Raise is reached via Steel Fell there is a high circuit of the Langdale Pikes; this leads to Bowfell and the Scafell Massif which includes the mauvais pas of Broad Stand before the long drop to Wasdale. Fourth, it follows the Rev Elliot's circuit over Pillar to Gable where it turns north over Brandreth to the Honister Pass. Finally the completion of Dale Head, Hindscarth and Robinson leaves four and a half miles of road back to Keswick.

Unless you are in the serious athlete class there are certain logistical considerations to take into account. To start with, which is the better direction to take? Most do it anti-clockwise, but there are advantages to be gained by doing it in the opposite direction. The Skiddaw section can be very tiring if done last; you ascend rather than descend the rock climb of Broad Stand and the last section with its reasonable ascent and considerable road work has the easiest and quickest going of all. This final point could act as a substantial morale booster. On the other hand, the orthodox get off to a flier which can put them in good heart and settle pre-match nerves. In the end, it must be a question of personal taste and temperament.

The next question is when do you attempt it and what time do you start? The answer to the first part is obvious - as near to the Summer Solstice as you can manage - to the second not so. If you are aiming to complete the round in a time approaching twenty-four hours you will have to travel in the dark. Where do you want to be when night falls? Or rather, where do you not want to be during the hours of darkness? The answers to these questions usually dictate your starting time. An alternative is to start and finish in the dark. It may not be irrelevant that Bob Graham set off at 1.00 am in a clockwise direction. Again, if you are the average attempter, you will have to give some thought to the course itself. It goes without saying that you or at least your support party can find the way blindfold. Most people break it down into sections and have split times, usually each summit and pass or valley, which they use to maintain an even pace. It is also common practice to have a fresh support party over each leg to achieve the same result. If your parties are strong and knowledgeable you do not have to think; you will be towed round.

It seems to me that such an approach misses one of the points of challenges of this sort. That is, you have the opportunity to rely on your own resources. To do it solo would be very difficult and arguably foolish but the spirit would be best captured if done with one or two companions who are making a simultaneous attempt. Under these circumstances, it is also very useful to do your training on the ground. Split times prepared by others are all very well in theory but when you know in practice that you have reduced your time over the same distance as compared to last week's attempt, it fuels your determination. This enables you to play psychological games with yourself. You allow yourself *x* minutes from A to B, although you know you can do it faster. There will be sections that are always recalcitrant; here you should give yourself a little leeway. If on the day these times improve, even by a minute or so, they will slowly add up to a respectable cushion. What you should not do is 'cheat' in training; there are a number of occasions when the summit lies just off the natural line of the hills being traversed and it is tempting to cut the corner and assume that you will make it up on the day. Hindscarth is a good example. The path runs directly from Dalehead to Robinson but the cairn on Hindscarth is on a spur off this direct line. It is only half a mile without any significant ascent but it is also half a mile back. You don't need many of these before your schedule is in tatters.

One of the reasons for the longevity of Bob Graham's record was that it appeared to the average person as superhuman. To run one marathon put you in an élite class of athletic legend; to run three and climb Mount Everest in a day seemed beyond comprehension. Before you have any chance of doing it you must break this barrier of self-doubt. There is in all of us a Hamlet that fears the 'undiscover'd country' and we could follow his example by attacking softer targets before addressing the real task. An example of such is a The Lakes from South to North. You start at Coniston and ascend The Old Man. You traverse the Coniston Fells via Swirl How and descend to Three Shire Stone in Wrynose Pass. Climb Cold Pike to reach the south arm of the Langdale Horseshoe and reach Bowfell over Crinkle and Shelter Crags. At this point you join the BGR which you can follow in either direction. If your choice is anti-clockwise, you will give yourself the longer option plus a sting in the tail. As you have done some work before Bowfell is reached, your time on the second leg could be a useful indicator of your state of preparedness.

The final ingredient is luck. Even in June the weather on the fells can be foul and a combination of rain and wind can be debilitating, as can 80° Fahrenheit between the hours of eleven and three. But, like the Prince of Denmark, we must accept that there is no point in worrying about the odd sparrow or two falling on our heads but acknowledge that

The readiness is all.

Yet the BGR and its ilk are only one of the games

that walkers play in the Lakes. Walking the fells is part of the normal life for many of the inhabitants and shepherds must have indulged in at least easy rock climbing to rescue cragfast sheep or in avoiding a tiresome detour. The competitive edge was given by the Guide Race which was a feature of the local 'Sports'. The original rules consisted of rowing a boat across the lake, running up and leaping down an adjacent fell and rowing back to the finish. All this was in full view of the spectators and often formed the climax to the day's events. In more recent times this has developed into a Fell Race which usually follows a round of about five miles.

The second sport of the fells consisted of chasing and, at times, catching small furry animals. I don't wish to enter into the hunting debate, but merely point out that there is considerably more furore about dogs chasing bunny rabbits than there is about dogs chasing rats. At the turn of this century, C E Benson recorded in his book *Crag and Hound in Lakeland* that there were eight fellside hunts. Because of the nature of the terrain, the huntsmen followed on foot and in the 'Hound' section of the book there is a full account of a day with the 'Blencathra' which gives an exact picture of what was involved. Benson's ultimate purpose is to persuade the reader towards the delights of rock-climbing and he sees his support of fox-hunting as a means to that end, as his final paragraph shows:

> *Rambling and scrambling is delightful; fox-hunting is better in that it supplies an object to one's rambles, to say nothing of the spirit of emulation and the joy of the chase; but the grandest sport of all is rock-climbing.*

However it was not necessary to kill anything to achieve 'the spirit of emulation and the joy of the chase'. As Benson himself states:

> *A hound trail, besides being exciting, is an exceedingly pretty sight, and well worth the watching.*

The scent is provided by a drag steeped in aniseed oil and laid down every quarter of a mile and pressed into the ground with the foot. The hounds are started from leash and the first home is the winner. The average trail was about eight miles long and would be completed in around twenty-five minutes. A human version of this is the sport of 'Hare and Hounds'. Here the Hares lay a trail of paper - or in these PC times wood-shavings - and after an appropriate start the Hounds or Pack follow, led by the Pacemaker and controlled by the Whip. Only when the Hares are sighted will the Whip unleash the pack who then individually try to overtake the pursued. The Macclesfield area plays host to the Cheshire Tally-Ho Hare and Hounds Club which was founded in 1872 and is still going strong. Although it travels far afield, many of the runs cover the same and similar ground as the walks described in Part One. It is interesting that the club rules suggest that 'The ordinary run shall not exceed eight miles.' Clearly this is the optimum distance for both man and beast.

Another human version of the hunt was a game played in the Lake District, introduced by Cambridge reading parties but refined by the climbing clubs into the sport of 'Scouts and Outposts'. In his collection of essays, *Heart of Lakeland*, L J Oppenheimer describes one such event. The aim was for five 'Scouts' to attempt to reach, in this case, the summit of Scafell Pike undetected by twenty-five 'Outposts' within a stated time. The 'Outposts' could go wherever they liked as long as they kept outside a threequarters of a mile radius of the summit. A 'Scout' would be assumed caught if he was simultanously spotted by two 'Outposts' each within a hundred yards of him. An 'Outpost' was incapacitated if touched by a 'Scout'. The two parties wore red and white sashes respectively. At the end, points were awarded for relative success and failure and a result was reached. All very North West Frontierish.

What is perhaps more interesting than the game itself is Oppenheimer's reaction to the overpopulation of England's highest summit. In addition to the thirty players there were as many tourists, picnicking, taking snapshots and misidentifying the local countryside. The author describes the scene in humorous detail and concludes:

> *Imagine this sort of thing kept on for nearly an hour, always a dozen people shouting at once, with occasional wild war whoops interspersed, and you may perhaps have some idea of the way we desecrated Sca Fell Pike that afternoon. It was a pleasant contrast (after going down to Wastdale for tea and to meet old friends) to have a quiet walk back to Rosthwaite with the Captain of the Outposts, under the sunset glow of the Napes, and then in the cool stillness of twilight down Borrowdale.*

This was written the best part of a century ago and casts another light on the subject of access. We all want access for ourselves but are not happy to have the place flooded with others; if Oppenheimer thought the Lakes were 'desecrated' then, what would he make of the present situation and, indeed, what do we make of the future?

More people are retiring early and they are living longer. They seek an activity which is economically and medically prudent. Hill-walking fits the bill. This is a substantial captive market, which naturally excites the greasy-till fumblers; unnecessary gear is foisted upon them and they are herded around the beaten tracks. At some point control is deemed necessary and Park Wardens are employed to direct the traffic. I had not realised their role until I encountered one in the car-park below the waterfall of Grey Mare's Tail. I had done a round of the Corbetts in the Moffat area and was returning to my starting point. I took what I assumed to be a sensible direct line but halfway down an awkward heather and boulder hillside realised that I would have been better advised to have contoured the corrie and descended by the stream. I eventually made my destination, to be greeted by an Officer of the Great Outdoors.

Off: Was that you coming down that hillside, Sir?
Me: Yes.
Off: Rather a foolish thing to do, don't you think, Sir?

(At this point he seemed to be making a critical appraisal of my not particularly waterproof waterproofs and the apparent absence of the obligatory half a hundred weight of survival equipment.)

Me: Yes. I can see there is a better way, now.
Off: In these parts, Sir, we advise people that it is good practice to keep to the paths. Enjoy the rest of your day.

I almost expected a click of the heels and an RAC type salute, but he merely returned to his duties of rounding up the squirrels which were cluttering the space demanded by a very big motor car.

If this type of control goes against the grain, yet we accept that some control is necessary, what form is it to take? I would not go so far as the élitist suggestion that The Nature Conservancy should build moats around all worthwhile mountains and fill them waist-deep with slurry, the only 'clean' point of access to

Great Calva
Skiddaw.
Blencathra
Threlkeld
Keswick
Clough Head.
Derwent Water.
The Dodds
Gillbarrow
Raise

Route Eight: The Bob Graham Round

be thirty-foot rockfaces at mild severe standard or harder. But the idea of a moat has possibilities. There would be an inner sanctum where no cars are allowed and an outer band where visitors, by the alternative of a stiff toll, would be encouraged to park and ride. This might persuade people to spread the load by seeking less popular places; longer walks in and out might tease out the congestion and, if it encouraged people to stay overnight rather than rush up and down motorways, the local economy would benefit.

As, according to a recent newspaper article, the whole population of the world would, if neatly stacked, fit into the space occupied by Lake Windermere, we are a long way from gridlock on the hills. Though I did see an interesting case where two parties attempting a girdle traverse in different directions were involved in a race between themselves and a climber on an orthodox ascent for the only available stance (very macramé that turned out to be). The danger is that we will take the easier path of procrastination and that it will never be a vote-catching issue for short-term politics to address. As successive governments have destroyed football as a communal activity by allowing and, by association, encouraging lawlessness on the grounds that 'at least we know where all the head-bangers are on a Saturday afternoon', I am tempted into feeling that there may be a similar conspiracy between The Landowners and The National Trust. The hope is that such organisations as The John Muir Trust will continue to rise above petty self-interest and act as a rallying point for those who really care.

In the immediate future, any idea that reduces car traffic is to be encouraged as it will lead to an increased demand for public transport. This demand would produce a better service and, more importantly, revive the concept of communal travel. Life at its best strikes a balance between privacy and social interaction and over-reliance on the car inhibits the latter. We live in the bubble of our house and drive the bubble car to other bubbles of work and play. This would not matter so much if it wasn't for the fact that these two modes of human behaviour also accord with the concepts of selfishness and selflessness. We all need a room of our own but when this induces a 'laager' mentality, social interaction is reduced to prejudice and intolerance.

I believe that people attracted to walking and climbing are inclined towards maintaining this balance; it is, after all, a pastime that you do by yourself in the company of others and where talking to strangers on the hill is the norm. One advantage of the 'grey vote' is that it has for the most part gone past selfish posturing and the 'I want it now and on my terms' approach and might be inclined to a more selfless view. If this lobby were to increase, as seems inevitable, a change of attitude may occur and we might become pro- rather than re-active. If not, public transport will remain the domain of the marginalised and public houses will become cafés with bolt-on play pens. As for the hills ...

Bibliography

Baddeley, M J B, *The Lake District* (Ward, Lock & Co)

Baker, E A, *Moors, Crags & Caves in the High Peak* (Heywood, 1903)

Benson, C E, *Crag and Hound in Lakeland* (Hurst & Blackett, 1902)

Borthwick, A, *Always a Little Further* (Faber, 1939)

Bowman, W E, *The Ascent of Rum Doodle* (Parish, 1956)

Byne, E & Sutton, G J S, *High Peak - The Story of Walking & Climbing in the Peak District* (Secker & Warburg, 1966)

Dawson, A, *The Relative Hills of Britain* (Cicerone Press, 1992)

Docharty, W A, *A Selection of 900 British and Irish Mountains* (privately published, 1954)

Dutton, G C E, *The Ridiculous Mountains* (Diadem, 1984)

Firbank, T, *I Bought a Mountain* (Harrop & Co, 1940)

Gripanpul, Brig E Q (Johnny), *Llà-Dos: The Last Lost Mountain* (Rockall Publications, 1913)

Hancock, G, *The Goyt (The Forgotten Valley) and Errwood Hall*

Hewitt, D, *Walking the Watershed* (TACit Press, 1994)

Jeuda, B, *The Macclesfield, Bollington & Marple Railway* (Cheshire County Council)

MacRab, J, *Some Scrambles Outwith the Scottish Mainland* (Smart Press, 1965)

Montague, C E, *A Botanist in Hanging Garden Gully* (Chatto & Windus)

Murray, W H, *Mountaineering in Scotland* (Dent, 1947)

Newton, Lady, *The House of Lyme* (Heinemann, 1917)

Oppenheimer, L J, *Heart of Lakeland* (Sherratt & Hughes, 1908)

Patey, T, *One Man's Mountains* (Gollancz, 1971)

Perrin, J, *Menlove* (Gollancz, 1985)

Sutton, G J S & Noyce, C W F, *Samson: the Life and Writings of Menlove Edwards* (Cloister Press, 1961)

Wilson, K & Gilbert, R, *The Big Walks* (Diadem, 1980)

About
The John Muir Trust

The root of this movement was the threat by the Ministry of Defence to purchase an area of the Knoydart peninsula, at one time owned by the brewer, Colonel Whitbread, and known to climbers as the Whitbread Wilderness. As the inevitable consequence would have been a severe restriction in access to one of the most attractive parts of the Highlands, there was a public outcry. This was picked up by the Press, who wrote indignantly about the right to roam and supported their appeal with a suitable selection of pictures showing the 'Celtic Twilight'. Under most circumstances, this would have been a three-day wonder and at this very moment the defenders of the nation would be practising their yomping to enable us to safeguard the 'cherished and traditional' interests of mineral companies operating in the South Atlantic.

However, on this occasion, words were translated into action and a group calling itself The John Muir Trust, after the founding father of the world conservation movement, bought, through public subscription, an important section of the Knoydart peninsula. Since 1983 the Trust has devoted itself to making Muir's message 'to do something for the wildness and make the mountains glad' a real possibility within Britain. Its aim is to acquire and intelligently manage significant wild areas, so that they can be enjoyed by generations to come.

As with all institutions, there will be a variety of views on the best way forward, but I feel that the basic premise deserves all the support it can get. Because it has started from scratch, without all the baggage of vested interest, it could become the model for land occupancy in the next century.

Further information may be obtained from:
The John Muir Trust
41 Commercial Street
Leith, Edinburgh, EH6 6JE.